MATTHEW

For
Cameron, Luke and Josh Holland

NAVIGATING THE GOSPELS

Matthew

Philip Fogarty SJ

the columba press

First published in 2010 by
the columba press
55A Spruce Avenue, Stillorgan Industrial Park,
Blackrock, Co Dublin

Cover by Bill Bolger
Origination by The Columba Press
Printed in Ireland by ColourBooks Ltd, Dublin

ISBN 978-1-85607-665-4

Table of Contents

Preface

People sometimes think of the gospels as biographies of Jesus, somewhat similar to the biographies of famous people written today. But, unlike modern biographies, the gospels tell us very little about Jesus' childhood, his family background, his education, or even what he looked like. What all the gospel writers were seeking to achieve can be summed up in the words of John's gospel: 'These things are written that you may believe that Jesus is the Messiah, the Son of God, and that believing you may have life in his name.' (John 20:31)

The word gospel comes from the Greek word *euaggelion* meaning 'good announcement' or 'good news'. Words related to it were often employed in non-Christian circles, especially in speaking of victory in battle. In the imperial cult, the emperor's birth and presence were said to be good news for the Roman world. For Christians the good news was Jesus' proclamation of the kingdom of God, or God's reign, as manifested in his life, death and resurrection.

Jesus attracted and convinced a large number of followers who, after his resurrection, went on to proclaim him throughout the known world. Major aspects of the actual life of Jesus, the Jesus who walked this earth, are unreported and thus unknowable. However, if one accepts that the portraits of Jesus in the gospels retain quite an amount of material from his life on earth, and that the missionary purpose of the gospel writers was not alien to his own, these portraits are as close to the 'real' Jesus as we are likely to get.

Most of us today cannot remember clearly what happened sixty or eighty years ago, and since the gospel writers were not contemporaries of Jesus, they had to rely on oral and written accounts of what Jesus said and did. Given the strong oral traditions of ancient peoples, such as could be found in Irish oral traditions even up to the last century, it is quite plausible that the evangelists could quote Jesus' sayings and deeds with some degree of accuracy, even if one allows for the religious and theological interpretations that they later imprinted on those same sayings and doings.

Three stages of development led up to the writing of the gospels. First of all there was what Jesus said and did. Jesus was a Jew who lived in Galilee and moved in and out of Jerusalem in the twenties. The language he spoke, his ways of thinking and acting, the problems he faced were those of a specific time and place. Gospel readers sometimes remove him from time and space, and imagine that he dealt with issues that he never in fact encountered.

For example, people ask such questions as to whether Jesus would have approved of the war in Iraq, or whether he could have foreseen that men would land on the moon. But Jesus, as a Galilean Jew, would not have known of the existence of Sadaam Hussein or of the existence of modern space travel. After all, 'he was like us in all things but sin.' What Jesus said and did, however, does have implications for questions concerning war and peace.

The second stage of development of the gospels consisted of the preaching of the apostles, those who had known and walked with Jesus before his death and resurrection. Since Jesus' mother tongue was Aramaic, and because he lived in a largely village culture, the apostles and other early preachers, like Saint Paul, had to 'translate' what he said and did from Jesus' culture into a wider Greek-speaking one.

After Jesus' resurrection his disciples came to understand him more fully as the one who most perfectly imaged God and God's love for Israel and the world. They saw him as the very presence of God in the world, and the resurrection lit up their understanding of what they had seen and heard during Jesus' ministry.

Now, however, they had to preach that Jesus to urban Jews and Gentiles in Greek, a language that Jesus did not normally speak. This involved adapting the vocabulary and patterns of speech that Jesus used in ways that would make the message alive for new audiences.

The final stage that led to the writing of the gospels was when a member of a particular Christian community (the evangelist) took material from the living tradition about Jesus and shaped it in such a way that it offered a basis of faith and morality to a particular audience, one that was largely Gentile.

The evangelists were not eye-witnesses who had walked the roads of Palestine with Jesus. Rather, as members of particular Christian communities that existed somewhere between the years 60 and 110AD, they arranged the material they had received in order to portray Jesus in a way that people could understand, and come to know, love and serve.

The designations one finds in the New Testament, such as 'The gospel according to Matthew', are the result of late-second-century scholars' attempts to identify the authors of works that had no identification. No gospel writer indicated who he was. The closest one comes to that in the gospels is the indication in John's gospel that an eyewitness, 'the disciple whom Jesus loved,' was the source of what is written in the gospel (John 21:24), but that gospel never identifies the beloved disciple.

Matthew's Gospel, written somewhere between 80 to 90 AD, became the church's Gospel par excellence and served as the foundational document of the church, rooted in the teaching of Jesus. The dominant influence it has had suggests that it was composed for a major Christian community in an important city such as Antioch in Syria, and was addressed in all probability to a Christian community that was once strongly Jewish but had become increasingly Gentile in composition.

The following pages, based on the insights of contemporary scripture scholars, and using the *New Revised Standard Version* of the gospels, are an attempt to offer some overall insights into the gospel. They are intended for the general reader who wishes to know how the gospel came to be written and what it has to tell us about Jesus who once walked the dusty roads of Palestine demonstrating God's love for humanity. Jesus is 'our everyday God' showing us how to live and die in a meaningful way. As St Paul said of him, 'though he was in the form of God, (he) did not regard equality with God as something to be exploited, but emptied himself taking the form of a slave.' (Philippians 2:6ff)

Jesus always had the nature of God. He never ceased being God. That would have been impossible. Instead he emptied himself, taking the form of a servant. He freely gave up all the prerequisites inherent in the divine omnipotence and the divine knowledge. To quote one author, 'To use a crude analogy, he became amnesiac so that he could learn and grow just as we do.'[1]

These pages should not replace reading and meditating on the gospel itself. While it is important to understand what the evangelist means, the reader is also invited to let the gospel speak to the heart as well as the head. There is an age-old tradition of contemplating the gospels, and so the reader is invited to undertake an imaginative journey, looking at the people, places and actions of the various actors in the gospel stories, identifying with them imaginatively in the hope of better appreciating each gospel's message.

We are familiar with the great variety of physical exercises, such as walking, jogging, and sports. These physical exercises are good for tuning up the body, improving circulation and breathing and the general overall good health of the body.

Spiritual exercises such as meditation or contemplation of the gospel stories increase our openness to the movements of God's Spirit in our hearts, and help us build a closer relationship with Jesus as we respond more fully to the love of God made manifest in him. John's gospel asks the basic questions that all the gospels put to us today: Do you believe? Do you love? Are you a disciple?

---

1. *God: The Oldest Question*, William J. O'Malley SJ, Loyola Press, Chicago, 2000.

CHAPTER ONE

Background

To appreciate the gospel of Matthew more fully, it is worthwhile beginning by saying something about the political situation in Palestine as it was over two thousand years ago when a small-town Jew, one Jesus of Nazareth, was born into a family of woodworkers.

It was a bad time for Jews. Their land had been occupied by a succession of conquerors, and these had diluted and even infected their culture. Alexander the Great, the Greek warrior king of Macedon, who ruled over a vast empire that enabled him to call himself 'Lord of Asia', conquered Samaria and Judea about 332 BC, and the Jews of the Palestine-Syria area became part of what we now call the Hellenistic world with its mixture of Greek and Roman culture.

By the time of Jesus' birth Rome was the dominant power. Roman occupation of Palestine began in 67BC. The Romans ruled Palestine by working through subservient high priestly rulers and kinglets. Herod the Great (37-4BC) was subservient to Rome but enjoyed full domestic autonomy. He did not have to pay tribute to Rome, but was subject to it in all matters of war and foreign policy. He was an unscrupulous schemer and a passionate autocrat, deeply influenced by Greek culture, with little interest in Judaism. Though King of the Jews, he was not a truly Jewish King. He was regarded with contempt by many Jewish subjects as only a half Jew. The brutal cruelty, and virtual insanity of his last years, gave rise to Matthew's account of the massacre of children two years and under in Bethlehem.[1]

The gospels of Mathew and Luke both refer to the birth of Jesus as occurring during the reign of Herod the Great.

---

1. Matthew 2:16ff

Assuming that the reference is accurate, it would appear that Jesus was born BC, 'before Christ'! He was born somewhere between 7 and 4BC, in the last years of Herod's reign. Dionysius Exiguus, a sixth-century monk, who created our dating system of BC and AD ('*Anno Domini*', in the year of the Lord) simply made a miscalculation on the basis of earlier calendar models.

When Herod died, the Emperor Augustus split the realm between his three sons. Archelaus was put in charge of Judea, Samaria and Idumea to the south of Palestine and Herod Antipas ruled Galilee in the north and part of the Transjordan. Philip ruled in the region east and north of the Lake of Galilee. Archelaus was so cruel that his subjects sent a delegation to Rome and had him removed. A Roman Governor, the well-known Pontius Pilate, replaced him.

Such was the political climate when Jesus was born in Bethlehem. His mother was called Miryam (Mary) and his putative father was called Yosef (Joseph) who, it was claimed, was a descendant of King David. Jesus grew up in Nazareth and was so identified with the town that he was later known as Jesus the Nazarene.

Jesus probably spoke Aramaic as his main language, though there is reason to believe that he knew biblical Hebrew and possibly some Greek, which was the language often used in trade in the bigger towns of the time. It is reasonable to suppose that his religious formation included instruction in reading biblical Hebrew.

As the first-born son, Jesus would have learned his father's trade but would also have been taught the religious traditions and texts of Judaism. His skill, as an adult, in debating with the Scribes, Pharisees and Jerusalem authorities argues for some degree of reading knowledge of the sacred texts. He may even have received some primary education in the synagogue in Nazareth.

If this is so, we can well understand the reaction of his peers and elders when he later returned to teach there. 'On the Sabbath he began to teach in the synagogue, and many who heard him were astounded. They said, "Where did this man get all this? What is this wisdom that has been given to him? What deeds of power are being done by his hands! Is not this the carpenter, the Son of Mary and the brother of James and Joses and Judas and Simon, and are not his sisters here with us?" And they took offence at him.'[2] In other words, 'who does he think he is?'

Jesus plied his trade as a woodworker. He would have done work in carpentry making beds, tables, stools and lamp-stands, ploughs and yokes, but he probably did some work in stone as well. While he would have had to work hard for his living, Jesus was probably no poorer or less respectable than anyone else in Nazareth or in the rest of Galilee for that matter. There is no reason to believe that he suffered from the grinding, degrading poverty of the day labourer or the rural slave. He worked as a tradesman, a calling involving a broad range of skills demanding much sweat and muscle power, hardly the weakling often presented in pious paintings.

So for the first thirty years of his life, Jesus lived an obscure life in Nazareth, a hill town of between one thousand six hundred and two thousand people. He was known simply as the woodworker's son. All in all, there was nothing in his early life or educational background that prepared his family, or his fellow townspeople, for the startling career that he undertook in his early thirties.

Many years later, somewhere between 80 and 90AD, a Greek speaker, probably a Jewish Christian, who knew Aramaic or Hebrew or both, but was not an eyewitness of Jesus' ministry, set out to tell the story of Jesus. He wrote his gospel in Greek probably somewhere in the Antioch region in what is now Syria. In a tradition dating back to the second century, Matthew, the tax collector, who became an apostle, was credited with the gospel's authorship.

However since the author of the final Greek text seems to have copied, with modifications, the whole of Mark's gospel, it

---

2. Mark 6:1-4

is now commonly thought improbable that, in its present form, it is the work of an eyewitness apostle. Why would an eyewitness need to copy from Mark who was not himself an eyewitness? Matthew the apostle may, however, have been at the start of the gospel tradition if he gathered Aramaic sayings of Jesus that were later used by the author.

As we begin to examine Matthew's gospel in some detail, it is worthwhile keeping the political scene that prevailed at the time in mind, as well as the little that we can say with any certainty about Jesus' upbringing and education.

Jesus' Origins
(1-2)

Things are not always what they seem. The infancy stories in the gospels of Matthew and Luke are a case in point. They seem, on the surface, to provide a simple and very attractive account of how Jesus came to be born in Bethlehem, and of the events immediately after his birth. But there are very noticeable differences in the two accounts.

According to Matthew's gospel, Mary and Joseph live in Bethlehem in Judea, and the wise men come to visit them in their home there.[1] After the flight into Egypt they do not return to Bethlehem because the tyrant Archelaus, King Herod's son, is now ruler there. Instead they go to live in Nazareth in Galilee.[2] In Luke's gospel Mary and Joseph live in Nazareth and only go to Bethlehem because 'the Emperor Augustus decreed that the whole world should be registered.'[3]

The scripture scholar Raymond E. Brown has pointed out that, apart from Matthew's account, there is no other known historical record of what must have been a most unusual astronomical phenomenon – a star rising in the East leading the Wise Men to Jerusalem, then reappearing and eventually coming to rest on Jesus' home in Bethlehem. Surely others in Jerusalem or in Bethlehem would have noticed such an unusual event and recorded it?[4]

Luke writes 'a decree went out from Emperor Augustus that all the world should be registered. This was the first registration and was taken while Quirinius was governor of Syria.'[5]

1. Matthew 2:11
2. Matthew 2:22-23
3. Luke 2:1
4. *Birth of the Messiah*, Raymond E. Brown, Doubleday
5. Luke 2:1-2

However, as Brown again points out, there never was a single census that covered the whole world under Augustus, and the census that took place under Quirinius occurred about ten years after the death of Herod and, presumably, therefore, after the birth of Jesus.

One would expect that what is narrated in the stories about Jesus' birth would agree with what is to be found in the body of the gospel. In the second chapter of Matthew, when the wise men came to King Herod, and he and the chief priests and the scribes learned about the birth of the King of the Jews, all Jerusalem was disturbed by the event. Yet when Jesus appears in his public ministry nobody seems to know much about him or expect anything from him.[6]

According to Luke, Elizabeth the mother of John the Baptist was a relative of Mary, Jesus' mother. Yet during Jesus' public ministry there is no suggestion of such a relationship. Indeed in the gospel of John the Baptist says of Jesus, 'I myself did not know him.' (1:33)

On the other hand there are points of agreement in the two infancy narratives. In both there is an annunciation: to Joseph in Matthew and to Mary in Luke. Both agree that Jesus was conceived without a human father – an astounding claim indeed. Both agree that Jesus was 'of the house of David,' that he was born in Bethlehem, and finally that Jesus' family settled in Nazareth.

While some scholars think that some of the events described in the infancy stories may not be historical, but are inserted to make theological points about Jesus, the points of agreement between the two accounts would suggest that they do contain some historical details.

So, to fully appreciate the intention of the gospel writers, it is important to remember that their primary concern is not to provide us with historical details. They are trying to sum up, in story form, the basic message of the Old Testament, and demonstrate how the ancient Jewish scriptures find their fulfilment in the person of Jesus.

---

6. Matthew 13:54-56

Let us turn now to Matthew's gospel which opens with what, to many people, is a very off-putting introduction: a genealogy.[7] What Matthew is trying to do is to place Jesus' birth within the context of all of Jewish history from the time of Abraham up to the birth of Jesus. Using groups of fourteen to make his point, he gives the impression that God made mathematically precise preparations for the coming of the Messiah. The first fourteen names mentioned are those of the patriarchs, the ancestors of Israel, people such as Abraham, Isaac, Jacob, and so on. The second fourteen are Israel's kings, especially Kings David and Solomon, and the last fourteen are simply unknowns from Israel's past who played a vital role in the coming of the Messiah.

Matthew is reminding us that Jesus is the heir to the virtues associated with the great ancestors of Israel. The unknown names in the genealogy are a reminder that the Messiah will preach to those who would not be considered important by the world's standards.

Going through the list of fathers and sons, the genealogy ends as follows: 'Eliud the father of Eleazar, and Eleazar the father of Matthan, and Matthan the father of Jacob, and Jacob the father of Joseph the husband of Mary, of whom Jesus was born, who is called the Messiah.'[8] Matthew does not state that Joseph is Jesus' father but prepares the way for the extraordinary manner of Jesus' conception.

The genealogy also includes the names of four women, Tamar, Rahab, Ruth and Uriah's wife Bathsheba. The first three women were not Israelites, and Bathsheba was not married to an Israelite. While the marriages of all four women were irregular, nonetheless they played an important part in God's plan for the coming of the Messiah. It has been speculated that Matthew had two purposes in mind for including these women. In the first place, if some non-Jews had played such a vital role among the

---

7. Matthew 1:1-17. Luke has a different account of Jesus' ancestry in chapter 3:23-38
8. Matthew 1:16

antecedents of the Messiah, so the Jewish readers of Matthew's gospel might find it easier to accept his mixed congregation of Jews and Gentiles. The irregular marriages of the women might also prepare Matthew's readers for the extraordinary way in which Jesus was conceived.

Mary is engaged to Joseph, but before they live together 'she is found to be with child from the Holy Spirit.' What does it mean to be with child from the Holy Spirit? The Spirit (or Breath) of God was seen as the source of all of creation and of all human life.[9] So, just as God created all that exists in the heavens and the earth, now, through the power of God's Spirit, Jesus is conceived in the womb of Mary by a particular, concrete, and special case of God's creative activity.

Joseph is dumbfounded. Here he is with a pregnant wife who, seemingly, has had an adulterous affair. As an observant Jew, he knows that the full penalty of the law for adultery is death by stoning. However, his sense of what the law of Moses commands is tempered by his compassion that prevents him from wanting to exact the full rigours of the law, so he plans to divorce Mary quietly. But an angel of the Lord appears to him in a dream,[10] and says, 'Joseph, Son of David, do not be afraid to take Mary as your wife, for the child conceived in her is from the Holy Spirit. She will bear a son, and you are to name him Jesus, for he will save his people from their sins.' Matthew adds that all this took place to fulfil what had been spoken by the Lord through the prophet: 'Look, the virgin shall conceive and bear a son, and they shall name him Emmanuel,' which means, 'God is with us.'[11]

No doubt Joseph is more perplexed than ever, but when he wakes up, he does as the angel of the Lord has commanded; he

---

9. Genesis 2:7

10. In the Jewish scriptures, the term 'angel' was a common designation for God communicating with human beings, often in the form of a dream.

11. The quotation is from Isaiah. 'Look, the young woman is with child and shall bear a son, and shall name him Emmanuel.' (7:14)

takes Mary as his wife, but has no marital relations with her until she has borne a son whom she names Jesus.[12]

The gospel goes on to tell the story of the arrival of some wise men, or astrologers (magi), from the East, coming to Jerusalem, asking 'Where is the child who has been born king of the Jews? For we observed his star at its rising, and have come to pay him homage?' (For Matthew the star was a sort of 'revelation' in the natural world, because Gentiles did not have the Jewish scriptures to guide them.) Herod, now in the closing years of his reign, gets to hear about these strangers in the city, and is frightened at what they are saying about a king of the Jews. Potential rivals are not to be tolerated, so he calls together all the chief priests and scribes and inquires of them as to where the Messiah is to be born. They tell him 'In Bethlehem of Judea'. So he points the wise men in the direction of Bethlehem, saying to them, 'Go and search diligently for the child; and when you have found him, bring me word so that I may also go and pay him homage.'

The star appears once more, and the wise men follow it until it stops over the place where the child is. They enter the house and see the child Jesus at home with Mary his mother, and they kneel down and pay him homage. Then, opening their treasure chests, they offer him gifts of gold, frankincense, and myrrh – gifts fit for a king. Then, having been warned in a dream not to return to Herod, they depart for their own country by another road.

Matthew sees the magi as representatives of the Gentile world in all its racial diversity coming to Christ from the East, Persia, Syria and Arabia, just as many Gentiles did when they joined Matthew's community.

Joseph now has another dream[13] in which God tells him to 'Get up, take the child and his mother, and flee to Egypt, and remain there until I tell you; for Herod is about to search for the child, to destroy him. Then Joseph gets up, takes the child and his mother by night, and goes to Egypt.' Joseph and his family

---

12. Matthew 1:24-25. The name Jesus, or Joshua, means 'God Saves.'
13. Matthew 2:13-15

stay in Egypt until the death of Herod. Matthew says that this is to fulfil the prophecy of Hosea, 'Out of Egypt I have called my son.'[14] The 'son', in Hosea's prophecy, is Israel, God's people, and the reference is to the Israelite experience of salvation, the exodus from Egyptian captivity. Matthew applies the quotation to Jesus in two senses: to Jesus as an individual and to Jesus as representing the people of Israel as a whole, for in him the people will find salvation, just as they did through Moses.

Matthew often uses Old Testament parallels in his story. Just as Joseph, of multi-coloured dream-coat fame, interprets dreams,[15] so does Joseph, Mary's husband. Pharaoh tries to slay all the male children of the Hebrews,[16] only to have one of them, Moses, escape and become the saviour of his people. The tyrant Herod, not wanting any rivals, orders the massacre of all male children two years and under in Bethlehem and its vicinity, but Jesus escapes and he, in his turn, becomes the new saviour of his people. While the story of the massacre of the children[17] may, or may not, be historical, Herod certainly acts in character. If it is true, the number of children killed may not have exceeded twenty or so, but nonetheless there would certainly have been cause for 'sobbing and loud lamentation'[18] by the children's parents.

When Herod dies, the angel of the Lord again appears in a dream and tells Joseph to take the child and his mother back to Israel. When Joseph hears that the cruel tyrant Archelaus is ruling over Judea in place of his father Herod, he is afraid to go back there. Being warned in a dream, he departs for the region of Galilee. There he makes his home in Nazareth.'[19] Matthew again tells us that this is so in order that 'what had been spoken through the prophets might be fulfilled, 'He will be called a Nazorean.'

---

14. Hosea 11:1
15. Genesis 40
16. Exodus 1:16
17. Matthew 2:13-18
18. Jeremiah 31:15
19. Matthew 2:22

In the opening two chapters of his gospel, Matthew is not simply concerned with historical details but, by using Old Testament references, tries to alert us as to who Jesus is. He presents Jesus as Son of Abraham, Son of God, Emmanuel (God with us), Son of David and the new Moses. In other words, as he starts his story, Jesus is presented as the all-round saviour figure.

John the Baptist
(3)

John the Baptist was something of a 'wild card' for the gospel writers. He was an independent Jewish prophet who may have encountered Jesus of Nazareth only once. His independent worth in the eyes of first century Jews is reflected in the fact that, even after his death, groups of his disciples continued to venerate him. They refused to become Christians, and even became a rival movement during the early Christian period. As a revered figure, the four gospel writers could not afford to ignore him and so they had to make him 'safe' as it were. Mark pictures him as a messenger preparing the way for Jesus. Luke makes him a relative of Jesus. In John he is simply a witness to Jesus, while in Matthew the Baptist recognises Jesus' dignity and publicly confesses his own inferiority to Jesus just before he baptises him.

There is a tantalizing theory that John the Baptist's father, Zechariah, may have been a Temple priest in Jerusalem. John may have turned his back on his father and on his filial duty of continuing the priestly line that ministered in the Temple, becoming instead an anti-establishment prophet in the Judean desert in 28AD.[1] Be that as it may, Matthew pictures John as a fiery prophet in clothing made of camel's hair, a leather belt around his waist, living on locusts and wild honey in the desert area around the river Jordan.

People from Jerusalem and the surrounding area flock to see this extraordinary figure and be baptised, thrilled, yet terrified no doubt, by his preaching about the fiery imminent judgement of God.[2] 'Repent, for the kingdom of heaven has come near,'

---

1. John P. Meier, *A Marginal Jew: Rethinking the Historical Jesus, Volume II,* Doubleday. 1994
2. Matthew 3:1-12

John thunders. Matthew then explains John's role. 'This is the one of whom the prophet Isaiah spoke, when he said, 'the voice of one crying out in the wilderness: Prepare the way of the Lord, make his paths straight.'[3]

Pharisees and Sadducees[4] now join the crowd at the Jordan and John now turns his attention to them. 'You brood of vipers! Who warned you to flee from the wrath to come? Bear fruit worthy of repentance.' The Jewish leaders who come to be baptised are told that they are no better than a bunch of snakes fleeing from the danger of fire! They are warned about the 'wrath to come,' God's imminent and final judgement that John presumes is just around the corner. If they do not repent, have a change of heart, mind and behaviour, God's wrath will overwhelm them.

'Do not presume to say to yourselves, 'We have Abraham as our ancestor;' for I tell you, God is able from these stones to raise up children to Abraham. Even now the axe is lying at the root of the trees; every tree therefore that does not bear good fruit is cut down and thrown into the fire.'

John knows that it will be difficult to change the hearts and minds of this 'brood of vipers.' They claim physical descent from Abraham, and this provides them with a collective consciousness of being 'the chosen people'. This chosen status is intended to provide them with trust in God's promises, but can also breed smug complacency. John shatters that complacency by saying that God can 'make children of Abraham' out of the very stones at their feet. Unless there is repentance descent from Abraham is meaningless.

In John's view, the danger is imminent. 'Even now the axe

____

3. Isaiah 40:3

4. The Pharisees were a religious-political group of devout Jews who emphasised the zealous and careful study of the written Mosaic Law, as well as oral traditions that went beyond the Law. The Sadducees were also a religious-political group but were drawn mainly from among aristocratic laymen and members of the high-priestly families. Generally speaking, they lacked a following among the common people. They rejected some of the beliefs favoured by the Pharisees, most notably the latter's belief in the resurrection of the body, and of angels. Relations among these groups were at times quite vicious.

lies at the root of the tree.' The tree is a symbol for each individual. 'Every tree that does not bear good fruit will be cut down and thrown into the fire.' Presumably the trees that bear good fruit will be spared. What is striking is that the Jewish leaders who come to John are those who seem well disposed and have taken the trouble to come for baptism. So John's shocking message is that, in the face of God's wrath, even the ostensibly devout are in danger unless they confess their sins; not only their individual sins but also the corporate sins of the chosen people who have gone astray and hence lost any assurance they might have of being justified on the day of judgement. Only the swift decision to accept John's baptism and to combine it with a profound change of inner attitude and external conduct can rescue the individual Jew from the 'fire' soon to come. Perhaps Matthew also had the destruction of Jerusalem and its Temple in AD70 in mind?

After these dire warnings, John says, 'I baptise you with water for repentance, but the one who is more powerful than I is coming after me; I am not worthy to carry his sandals. He will baptise you with the Holy Spirit and fire. His winnowing fork is in his hand, and he will clear his threshing floor and will gather his wheat into the granary; but the chaff he will burn with unquenchable fire.' John never says who the more powerful one is. For Matthew, of course, it is Jesus. John's warning about the wheat and the chaff, reminds us of the parable of the Judgement of the Nations where God separates the good and the bad, and assigns them to their different fates.[5]

Jesus now appears on the scene. He comes from Galilee to the Jordan to be baptised by John. John tries to dissuade him. 'I need to be baptised by you, and do you come to me?' he says. But Jesus answers him, 'Let it be so for now; for it is proper for us in this way to fulfil all righteousness.'

As soon as Jesus is baptised by John, he comes up from the water, and suddenly the heavens open, and he sees the Spirit of God descending like a dove and alighting on him. A voice

---

5. Matthew 25:31ff

speaks from heaven, 'This is my Son, the Beloved, with whom I am well pleased.'

The story of Jesus' baptism is mentioned in all four gospels, but it was, in a way, something of an embarrassment for the early church because it was thought unsuitable that the sinless Jesus should be baptised. Matthew simply omits the reference in Mark's gospel to baptism being 'for the repentance for sins'.[6] Jesus allows himself to be baptised in order 'to fulfil all righteousness.' To 'fulfil' was the prophetic way of speaking about the fulfilment of prophecy, and 'righteousness' referred to moral conduct in conformity with God's will. What Matthew means is that Jesus is submitting himself to the plan of God for the salvation of the human race. This involves Jesus' identification with sinners, and for this reason it is appropriate for him to be baptised by John.

After Jesus comes up from the water 'he sees the Spirit of God coming upon him like a dove.' Matthew implies that this was a private experience of Jesus himself. A dove, a symbol of God's Spirit, descends on him, anointing him as Messiah. The words 'This is my Son, the Beloved, my favour rests on him', refer back to something that the prophet Isaiah wrote about the Suffering Servant, Israel: 'Here is my servant whom I uphold, my chosen, in whom my soul delights; I put my spirit upon him; he shall bring forth justice to the nations.'[7] Now, Matthew implies, Jesus is to be the Suffering Servant of God, and only in this humble sense the Messiah.

---

6. Mark 1:4
7. Isaiah 42:1

Jesus begins his Ministry
(4:1-25)

Before setting out on his ministry, Mark's gospel tells us that Jesus spends forty days being tempted, or tested, by Satan in the desert. He does not give us any details.[1] This is understandable since temptation is essentially a personal, inner experience, and so the gospel writers could not have known what went on in Jesus' mind and heart as he fasted in the wilderness.

Matthew's version, using Old Testament imagery, is an *interpretation*, in dramatic form, of the temptations that Jesus would encounter during his ministry, spelt out in such a way as to make them 'speak' to early Christian believers, Jews and Gentiles alike.

The book of Deuteronomy speaks of the Israelites wandering in the desert: 'Remember the long way that the Lord your God has led you these forty years in the wilderness, in order to humble you, testing you to know what was in your heart, whether or not you would keep his commandments.'[2] This passage provides the backdrop for Matthew's interpretation when he tells us that 'Jesus was led by the Spirit into the wilderness to be tempted by the devil. He fasted forty days and forty nights, and afterwards he was famished.'

The tempter comes and says to Jesus, 'If you are the Son of God, tell these stones to turn into loaves.' This is more than a straightforward temptation to turn stones into bread, or make the rock-filled Judean desert into a bakery! Jesus is tempted to turn stones into bread for his own personal convenience. He is being tempted to act out of self-interest. He answers his tempter, 'One does not live by bread alone, but by every word that comes

---

1. Mark 1:12
2. Deuteronomy 8:2

from the mouth of God.'[3] God's word is Jesus' primary nourishment, and the inspiration for all that he does.

Then the tempter takes him to Jerusalem and places him on the pinnacle of the temple, saying to him, 'If you are the Son of God, throw yourself down; for it is written, "He will command his angels concerning you," and "On their hands they will bear you up, so that you will not dash your foot against a stone".' Jesus says to him, 'Again it is written, "Do not put the Lord your God to the test".'[4] Jesus refuses to test God by demanding of him any extraordinary show of power.

Next the tempter takes him to a very high mountain and shows him all the kingdoms of the world and their splendour; and he says to Jesus, 'All these I will give you, if you will fall down and worship me.' Jesus replies, 'Away with you, Satan! For it is written, "Worship the Lord your God, and serve only him".'[5] Jesus rejects the temptation to worship power and wealth in place of worshipping and loving God with a unified heart.

These three temptations are reflected in Jesus' ministry. In John's gospel, the crowd reacts to the multiplication of the loaves by trying to make Jesus an earthly king,[6] and by seeking easily obtained bread.[7] The brothers of Jesus want him to leave the 'backwoods' of Galilee and go to Judea where he can show himself off to the world.[8] As he prepares himself for his public ministry, Jesus' temptations are aimed at diverting him from proclaiming God's kingdom, and replacing it with a kingdom based purely on worldly standards.

As Jesus begins his ministry, he hears that John the Baptist has been arrested. So, seeking greater safety, he leaves Nazareth and makes his home in Capernaum, a lakeside town on the borders of Zebulun and Naphtali, old tribal names for parts of

---

3. Deuteronomy 8:3
4. Deuteronomy 6:16
5. Deuteronomy 6:13
6. John 6:15
7. John 6:26-27
8. John 7:1-9

Palestine. In Matthew's day, Galilee was at least half Gentile in population, half pagan in cult, and bilingual – the population spoke Greek as well as Aramaic. By the time he wrote his gospel, many Gentiles formed part of the Christian community. Hence the relevance of Matthew's quotation from the prophet Isaiah: 'Land of Zebulun, Land of Naphtali, on the road by the sea, across the Jordan, Galilee of the Gentiles – the people who sat in darkness have seen a great light, and for those who sat in the region and shadow of death light has dawned.'[9] In Matthew's view, Jesus was now the great light for both Jews and Gentiles alike.

Jesus proclaims, 'Repent, for the kingdom of heaven[10] has come near.' These solemn words formally inaugurate Jesus' ministry. They are similar to those used by John the Baptist.[11] The central message of Jesus' preaching is the imminent coming of the kingdom of heaven, God's reign or rule, that will come about when people repent, have a complete change of heart, mind and conduct, turn away from sin, and carry out God's will as proclaimed by Jesus. The inevitable coming of the kingdom of God, when God will finally establish justice and peace on earth, forms the basis of Christian hope.

The idea for such a kingdom probably derives from the words of the prophet Daniel: 'As I watched in the night visions, I saw one like a human being coming with the clouds of heaven. And he came to the Ancient One and was presented before him. To him was given dominion and glory and kingship that all peoples, nations, and languages should serve him. His dominion is an everlasting dominion that shall not pass away, and his kingship is one that shall never be destroyed.'[12] For Matthew, the mysterious 'one like a human being' is, of course, Jesus.

---

9. Isaiah 9:1-2
10. Matthew, out of reverence, tends to avoid the direct mention of God. So, unlike Mark and Luke, he speaks of the 'kingdom of heaven'. This is perhaps unfortunate as it can mislead people into thinking that God's kingdom will exist only 'in heaven' and not here on earth.
11. Matthew 3:2
12. Daniel 7:13-14

While living in Capernaum, Jesus calls his first disciples. As he is walking by the Sea of Galilee, he sees two brothers, Simon, whom he will later call Peter, and his brother Andrew; they are casting in the lake with their nets, for they are fishermen. And he says to them, 'Follow me, and I will make you fish for people.'[13] And they leave their nets at once and follow him. As he sets off with Peter and Andrew he comes across two other brothers, James and John, sons of Zebedee, who are mending their nets. Jesus calls them too, and like Peter and Andrew, leaving the boat and their father, they follow him.

One has to wonder why these brothers would pack up and follow Jesus so easily. Perhaps, over time, they had already heard something about this charismatic preacher, and felt honoured to be asked to be part of his mission.

With his new friends, Jesus travels throughout Galilee, teaching in the synagogues, proclaiming the good news of the kingdom, and curing every disease and every sickness among the people. So his fame spreads and they bring to him all the sick, those who were afflicted with various diseases, demoniacs, epileptics, and paralytics, and he cures them. No wonder that great crowds follow him from Galilee, the Decapolis,[14] Jerusalem, Judea, and from beyond the Jordan. All told, even in these early days of his ministry, Matthew depicts Jesus as having a very wide sphere of influence.

---

13. Speaking about God restoring the people of Israel to their own land, Jeremiah, wrote, 'I am now sending for many fishermen, says the Lord, and they shall catch them.'
14. Ten Hellenistic towns in southern Syria.

The Beatitudes
(5:1-43)

Did Jesus once trudge up a mountainside and deliver the sermon that we now know as the Sermon on the Mount? No! Matthew gathered sayings of Jesus, as well as elements from the Psalms and from the prophet Isaiah,[1] and wove them into a sermon that encapsulates Jesus' teaching about the kingdom of God.

Jesus has attracted large crowds by his authoritative preaching and by his unusual powers of healing. They must be very surprised indeed when Jesus announces that the poor, the persecuted, and the hungry are a blessed lot! Empty stomachs, persecution and poverty hardly make for a very happy life. So what are we to make of Jesus' words?

'Blessed are the poor in spirit, for theirs is the kingdom of heaven.' Matthew's community was made up of people who were not poor or hungry, but he wanted them to know that Jesus reaches out to them also – provided that they have attitudes attuned to the kingdom of God or, in other words, that they are detached from their wealth, and are willing to share it with those in need.

'Blessed are those who mourn, for they will be comforted.' Jesus' words reflect those of the prophet Isaiah who spoke about his being sent to comfort all who mourn in Zion.[2] Jesus' disciples mourn because of the evils prevalent in Israel, and in the world generally, as well as the trials they are undergoing.

'Blessed the meek, for they will inherit the earth.' This is a reference to Psalm 37:11, 'The meek shall inherit the land, and delight in abundant prosperity.' The meek are those who are

---

1. Isaiah 61:1-4
2. Isaiah 61:1-3

'slow to anger' and 'gentle with others'. The meek will receive their reward when the fullness of God's kingdom comes about.

'Blessed are those who hunger and thirst for righteousness, they will be filled.' The background to this beatitude is Psalm 107: 'Let them thank the Lord for his steadfast love, for his wonderful works for humankind. For he satisfies the thirsty, and the hungry he fills with good things.' Those who seek God's righteousness, God's justice, are like the hungry Israelites who wandered in the desert and were fed by God. So those who hunger and thirst for justice, especially for the poor, will find ultimate satisfaction.

'Blessed the merciful, for they will receive mercy.' This is a blessing for those who pardon others, and are merciful especially towards the poor, because, as the book of Proverbs puts it, 'Those who mock the poor insult their Maker.'[3]

'Blessed are the pure in heart, for they will see God.' This is not a reference to sexual purity, nor to single mindedness, but to people of integrity, those who are morally upright. The background of the saying is to be found in Psalm 24: 'Who shall ascend the hill of the Lord? And who shall stand in his holy place? Those who have clean hands and pure hearts, who do not lift up their souls to what is false, and do not swear deceitfully.'

'Blessed are the peacemakers, for they will be called children of God.' While all true peace (*Shalom*) has its origins in God, followers of Jesus are called upon to be instruments of God's peace.

'Blessed are those who are persecuted for righteousness sake, for theirs is the kingdom of heaven.' Jesus' followers are considered righteous. Because their belief in Jesus' resurrection and divinity sets them apart from traditional Judaism, they are persecuted. So Jesus' words would certainly have comforted Matthew's readers at a time when they were being ostracised in Jewish society.

'Blessed are you when people revile you and persecute you and utter all kinds of evil against you falsely on my account. Rejoice and be glad, for your reward is great in heaven, for in the

---

3. Proverbs 17:5

same way they persecuted the prophets who were before you.' His followers can expect to suffer the same fate as Jesus. However, they can also afford to rejoice because, like Jesus, they will receive their reward when God's kingdom is realised in all its fullness.

Blessed are the unhappy ones, Jesus seems to be saying! Even now, the poor, the weak, the persecuted and the mournful are blessed not because they are morally better than others, but because God has a special care for them, rather like a mother who gives special care and attention to her sick child without, of course, loving any of her other children less.

Jesus himself demonstrated God's care and compassion for the powerless all during his ministry, and he now proposes to his disciples that they do the same. He speaks on behalf of the poor and marginalised who need to be reminded that God loves them, demonstrated by Jesus' suffering with them and for them. Jesus also addresses the powerful, those who need to be goaded by the example of those who have abandoned their comfort, (the 'poor in spirit,') and become champions of the downtrodden and the powerless. To be one with the poor, defend their undefended interests, be sympathetic and forgiving towards them, make peace when one can; these are the things, Jesus says, that make a person truly happy, truly blessed.

Having presented his manifesto, as it were, Jesus goes on to spell out some of its implications. Those who wish to follow him must be 'the salt of the earth' and a 'light to the world' so that, seeing their good deeds, others may give praise to God who makes such deeds possible.

Jesus reassures his Jewish audience that he did not come to abolish the law of Moses but to fulfil it. His argument is with the Scribes and Pharisees and their way of interpreting the law. After quoting a saying from scripture, Jesus would often qualify his opponents' interpretation: 'You may think this means' … 'but I say to you.' So he says, for example, not only is murder forbidden, but anger and insults as well because they can lead to rage, murder or other forms of violence. Anger, insults and retaliation must give way to reconciliation and love of one's enemies. 'So when you are offering your gift at the altar, if you remember that your brother or sister has something against you, leave your gift there before the altar and go; first be reconciled to your brother or sister, and then come and offer you gift.' How many Christians, one wonders, who attend church on a Sunday morning, take Jesus' words to heart?

Jesus says, 'You have heard that it was said, "You shall not commit adultery." But I say to you that everyone who looks at a woman with lust has already committed adultery with her in his heart.' Using Oriental hyperbole, Jesus continues, 'If your right eye causes you to sin, tear it out and throw it away; it is better for you to lose one of your members that for the whole body to be thrown into hell. And if your right hand causes you to sin, cut it off and throw it away; it is better for you to lose one of your members that for your whole body to go into hell.' Not only is adultery out of the question, those lustful intentions that lead to it are evil as well.

Jesus even forbids what Jewish law allowed, divorce. 'It has also been said: "Anyone who divorces his wife must give her a writ of dismissal." But I say this to you: everyone who divorces his wife, except for the case of fornication, makes her an adulteress; and anyone who marries a divorced woman commits adultery.' What does Jesus mean by allowing divorce 'except for the case of fornication'? The so-called Greek Orthodox solution holds that the clause speaks of adultery, and that it contains a real exception to the absolute prohibition of divorce and second marriage. But other sayings of Jesus about divorce prohibit it absolutely.[4] What Jesus is referring to here is a violation of the Mosaic law that forbids marriages between persons of certain blood and/or legal relationships.[5] Marriages of that sort were regarded as incest and hence invalid.

To understand Matthew, it is important to realise that, in

---

4. Mark 10:11-12; Luke 16:18. cf also 1 Corinthians 7:10-11b
5. Leviticus 18:6-18

Israelite law, men could divorce their wives on a whim[6] and an adulterous woman was in principle punished with death by stoning.[7] Since the whole question of divorce is often painful, it is useful to remember that Jesus' intent was not to cause pain. He sets out a clear and high ideal of human relations, a vision of marriage as a covenant of personal love between spouses which reflects the covenant relationship of God and his people. Unfortunately this vision does not always fit the vagaries of the human heart.

Speaking about retaliation, Jesus says, 'You have learnt how it was said: "an eye for eye and a tooth for a tooth".[8] But I say to you, do not resist an evildoer. But if anyone strikes you on the right cheek, turn the other too.' Striking the right cheek with the back of the hand was considered particularly dishonourable among Jews. Jesus seems to be saying that if one is insulted by a slap on the cheek, one should simply turn away and not retaliate. While Jesus condemns the use of physical violence, he always leaves open the possibility of psychological or moral resistance.

He says, 'You have heard that it was said, "You shall love your neighbour and hate your enemy".' Here Jesus is attacking a false interpretation of the Old Testament since it never commanded hate for one's enemies. 'But I say to you, love your enemies and pray for those who persecute you, so that you may be children of your Father in heaven; for he makes his sun rise on the evil and on the good, and sends rain on the righteous and on the unrighteous.' This is not hopeless idealism but a strategy for

---

6. The rabbinic school of Hillel says: 'He may divorce her even if she spoiled a dish for him, for it is written, 'because he has found in her indecency in anything.'

7. cf John 8:1-11

8. Before the development of juridical systems, Judaism allowed a limited form of violence to avoid unleashing a contagious cycle of reciprocal violence. 'An eye for an eye' was seen as preferable to the slaughter of a whole tribe because of some injury done to one individual. The Old Testament command, therefore, was meant to moderate vengeance: the punishment must not exceed the injury done.

overcoming one's persecutor: it is Jesus' strategy for winning. The goal is to try to shame one's opponent into a change of heart.

Jesus sets very high ideals for his disciples. Just as the Father causes his sun to rise on bad men as well as good, and his rain to fall on honest and dishonest people alike, so the disciples are to be perfect as God is perfect by loving enemies as well as friends. What Jesus proposes in the Beatitudes, and taught throughout his public life, certainly went against the grain of the ethical standards of the majority of societies in the ancient world, not to mention the ethical standards of our own time!

CHAPTER SIX

Alms, Prayer and Fasting
(6:1-7:28)

Having enunciated his basic programme in the Beatitudes, Jesus goes on to provide some comments on Jewish pious practices. 'Be careful not to parade your good deeds before men to attract their notice; by doing this you will lose all reward from your Father in heaven. So when you give alms, do not have it trumpeted before you; this is what the hypocrites do in the synagogues and in the streets to win men's admiration. I tell you solemnly, they have had their reward.' In other words, hypocrites desire praise and, if they receive what they are looking for, that is as much as they going to get. Jesus also applies the same lesson to fasting.

'When you pray, do not imitate the hypocrites; they love to say their prayers standing up in the synagogues and at the street corners for people to see them. I tell you solemnly, they have had their reward. But when you pray, go into your private room and, when you have shut the door, pray to your Father who is in that secret place and your Father who sees all that is done in secret will reward you.' Given the very different climate that exists in today's world, Jesus might well say the opposite, 'Pray in public'! Let your light shine before others so that, seeing you pray, they may be drawn to God.

Jesus gives his disciples an example of sound prayer using the familiar words of the Our Father. Matthew's version is more elaborate than the probably more original version used by Luke[1] where Jesus addresses God simply as 'Abba' (My Dear Father). Matthew has shaped the Lord's Prayer partially along the lines of synagogue prayer, and so he uses the more reverential 'Our Father in heaven' because he was troubled by the intimate famil-

---

1. Luke 11:2-4

iarity of greeting God as 'Abba'. Matthew, like most Jews, did not like to speak the name of God directly so, for example, he speaks of the kingdom of heaven where other evangelists speak of the kingdom of God: both terms meaning the same thing.

'May your name be held holy', 'your kingdom come', 'your will be done on earth as in heaven', are different ways of asking God to establish his kingdom in all its fullness. God's rule is already established in heaven and these petitions ask that it be established on earth. The kingdom is often portrayed in the Old and New Testaments using the image of a feast[2] and so the petition 'Give us today our daily bread' is a petition for the speedy coming of the heavenly banquet, the kingdom. The petition may also refer to the daily needs of those who are poor as well as to the Eucharist, a foretaste of the heavenly banquet.

'Forgive us our debts, as we have forgiven those who are in debt to us.' The coming of the kingdom will involve judgement on how people behave, and so the petitioner asks forgiveness in so far as he or she has not forgiven others. 'Debts' is a euphemism for sins: from whatever separates one from God or damages one's relationships with others. 'If you forgive others their failings, your heavenly Father will forgive you yours; but if you do not forgive others, your Father will not forgive your failings either.'

'Do not put us to the test,' or 'Do not subject us to the final test.' Some Jewish apocalyptic writings spoke of a dangerous struggle before the end of the age and so the petitioner asks to be spared that final test and to be delivered from the wiles of the evil one (Satan).

The remainder of Jesus' words speak of how his followers should deal with worldly possessions and the attitudes they should have if God's reign is to take hold of their hearts. They must be clear sighted so that the basic orientation of their lives is sound by being enlightened by Jesus' teaching. In this way they will store up incorruptible treasures in heaven. They are not to try to serve both God and Mammon (money or wealth). One

---

2. Isaiah 25:6; Matthew 8:11 and 22:1-10; Luke 13:29 and 14:15-24

cannot serve God with a divided heart but rather by making a decision to love God above all other things and all other things in so far as they fit into that basic love.

When Jesus says, 'Do not worry about your life, what you will eat or drink, or about your body, what you will wear', he is not referring to people who are destitute but rather to people who are relatively well-off. People should not make food and drink, one's body or one's clothes into idols or fetishes. Rather, Jesus says, 'Set your hearts on his kingdom first, and on his righteousness, and all these other things will be given to you.' In Matthew's gospel, seeking God's kingdom and seeking justice (righteousness) are not two distinct quests. There is no authentic search for the kingdom except in a quest whose immediate goal is God's justice: justice here on earth that makes a real difference in peoples lives, especially those who are poor.

'Do not judge, and you will not be judged' (by God). Jesus' followers are not to be everyone's conscience or censor. In adult life we cannot escape the obligation to make some judgements even on the moral character of others. Parents, teachers, employers and judges have to do this all the time. However, Jesus' teaching warns against usurping the definitive judgement of God, who alone sees into the human heart. Our judgement of others should always be tentative, partial and inadequate.

'Do not give dogs what is holy; and do not throw your pearls in front of pigs, or they may trample them and turn on you and tear you to pieces.' Dogs and swine were regarded as ritually unclean animals in Old Testament times. Jesus is telling his followers not to preach to those who are unsympathetic or hostile to his teaching since they would treat it with contempt, and the disciples might well be manhandled.

Jesus returns to the question of prayer. 'Ask and it will be given to you; search and you will find; knock, and the door will be opened to you.' But we do ask, seek and knock, and our prayers are not always answered. Of course what we ask for may not always be in our own best interests, or further God's kingdom. Rather the Father gives 'good things to those who ask him,' answering the deepest desires of the heart that people are often unable to articulate.

Jesus ends with some pithy advice: 'Enter through the narrow gate (Jesus himself); for the gate is wide and the road is easy that leads to destruction, and there are many who take it. For the gate is narrow and the road is hard that leads to life, and there are few who find it.' The way of discipleship leading to God's kingdom is demanding, but other ways lead only to spiritual death.

Miracles and Would-Be Followers
(8 and 9)

Stopping storms, curing blindness and leprosy, exorcising demons, raising the dead: I can hear it now – 'Come on, get real!' People either consign such marvels to the realm of fairy tales and the superstitions of pre-scientific peoples, or take a more moderate view that there 'may be something there' – incidents that originally made perfectly good scientific sense, but to which the gospel writers later added wondrous explanations.

However, the fact that Jesus performed extraordinary deeds, deemed by himself and others to be miracles, is so widely attested by the end of the first Christian generation, even by Josephus, a non-Christian historian, that we cannot simply set aside this aspect of his ministry. If the miracle tradition from Jesus' public ministry were to be rejected as completely unhistorical, so should every other gospel tradition about him. As someone said, 'For those who believe in God, no explanation is necessary. For those who do not, no explanation is possible.'

Having shown Jesus as a great preacher, Matthew's gospel goes on to present him as a doer of great deeds, and tells us of the many miracles he performed. He cleanses a leper[1] and a Centurion's servant,[2] thus breaking with his usual procedure of only ministering to Israelites, and anticipating the Christian mission to the Gentiles. Jesus cures Peter's mother-in-law,[3] he stills a storm,[4] heals two demoniacs,[5] a paralytic,[6] an official's daugh-

---

1. Matthew 8:1-4
2. Matthew 8:5-13
3. Matthew 8:14-17
4. Matthew 8:23-27
5. Matthew 8:28-43
6. Matthew 9:2-8

ter,[7] two blind men,[8] and a mute person.[9] Interjected between these miracle stories are other incidents about would-be followers of Jesus, the call of Matthew and a question about fasting.

Jesus, the healer-saviour, uses his miracles not as an attention-getting device but as a way of bringing about God's reign, God's kingdom, by demonstrating in practice God's love, compassion and power to heal and save his people.

There is frequent mention of 'possession' by demons in the gospel. Medical knowledge in the first century Mediterranean world was rather primitive. Mental illness, psychosomatic diseases, and such afflictions as epilepsy were often attributed to demonic possession. If Jesus saw himself called to battle against such evils, it was quite natural for him, as a first century Jew, to understand this dimension of his ministry in terms of exorcism. All of this simply underscores the obvious: Jesus was a man and a Jew of his time.

Matthew tells the strange story of the cure of two demoniacs in the territory of the Gadarenes, a largely non-Jewish area, more than thirty miles southeast of the Sea of Galilee.[10] Matthew's version is based on a longer version in Mark's gospel.[11] Two demoniacs come out of the tombs to meet Jesus. They are so fierce that people are scared to pass that way. Suddenly they shout, 'What have you to do with us, Son of God? Have you come here to torment us before the time?'[12] A large herd of pigs is feeding at some distance from them. The demons beg him, 'If you cast us out, send us into the herd of swine.' Jesus says to them, 'Go!' So they come out of the two demoniacs and enter the swine; and suddenly the whole herd rush down the steep bank into the sea and perish in the water. The swineherds run off and, going into town, they tell the whole story about what had happened with the demoniacs.

---

7. Matthew 9:18-26
8. Matthew 9:27-31
9. Matthew 9:32
10. Matthew 8:28ff
11. Mark 5:1-20
12. 'Before the time' reflects the idea that demons were free to trouble humanity until the end of time.

Then the whole town come out to meet Jesus; and when they see him, they beg him to leave their neighbourhood.

This story is the closest that the gospels come to comic story telling! To the Jews, pigs were unclean animals. For Gentiles, the Jew's horror of swine was a subject of laughter and teasing. However, the Gentile pig owner who lost his flock would hardly have been amused by the whole incident. Jesus probably performed an 'exorcism', a healing, in the Gadarene region and Mark, the first gospel writer to relate the story, elaborated on the incident by amusingly and symbolically having the unclean spirits go into the unclean pigs. The fact that a Gentile owned the pigs would not have been lost on Mark either. Matthew uses the same story in his gospel but shortens it considerably.

Matthew takes another 'miracle' story from Mark: the calming of the storm at sea. Matthew's version is again much shorter, and slightly different, from Mark's. Jesus gets into a boat and his disciples follow him. A violent storm comes up on the sea and the boat is nearly swamped by waves. Jesus is asleep. The disciples wake him and say, 'Lord, save us! We are perishing!' Jesus says to them, 'Why are you terrified, O you of little faith?' Jesus rebukes the winds and sea, and there is a great calm. The men are amazed and say, 'What sort of man is this, whom even the winds and sea obey?'

To understand the story one should consider some Old Testament passages, in particular the story of Jonah.[13] Jonah, fleeing from God, wants to go to the city of Tarshish. He goes aboard a ship and falls fast asleep in the hold. A furious storm blows up and the crew are frightened. The captain rouses Jonah and he is blamed, and accepts blame, for the storm. They throw him into the sea and pray to Jonah's God. Then the storm abates.

In Matthew's story, instead of Jonah fleeing from God, there is Jesus who is totally obedient to God's will. As Messiah and Son of God, Jesus does not have to pray to Israel's God. Rather, with the power that the Old Testament ascribes to God, Jesus himself stills the wind and sea, and rebukes the disciples for

---

13. The Book of Jonah 1:1-15

their lack of faith. Mark and Matthew's story may well have been a reworking of the Jonah story by the early church, to demonstrate how the Risen Jesus is Lord and Master even of the elements.[14]

Matthew then relates two stories about would-be followers. A scribe approaches Jesus and says to him, 'Teacher, I will follow you wherever you go.' Jesus says to him, 'Foxes have holes, and birds of the air have nests; but the Son of Man has nowhere to lay his head.' The scribe indicates that he wants to be a disciple. Jesus replies that if the scribe wants to be a true follower he will have to be prepared to undertake a risky, unsettled, itinerant way of life.

Another disciple says to Jesus, 'Lord, first let me go and bury my father.' But Jesus says to him, 'Follow me, and let the dead bury their own dead.' The saying is probably to be taken as deliberate hyperbole intended to shock his hearers. In the Jewish and Hellenistic worlds there was no higher filial duty than burying one's dead father. Jesus' harsh reply must have sounded intentionally shocking to his audience as he says, in effect, 'Let those who refuse to accept God's reign, the spiritually dead, bury the physically dead.' Following Jesus and sharing his mission of preaching and healing, can override even the most solemn of obligations.

As Jesus walks along, he sees a man called Matthew sitting at a tax booth; and he says to him, 'Follow me,' and he gets up and follows him. Matthew must have had some prior knowledge of Jesus and his mission, and have given some thought to following Jesus, otherwise why would he just get up and follow this itinerant teacher?

Jesus then goes to dinner in Matthew's home. Other tax collectors and sinners sit with him and with the disciples. When the Pharisees see this, they say to the disciples, 'Why does your teacher eat with tax collectors and sinners?' Jesus says, 'Those

---

14. Psalm 107 (23-30) may also have been part of the background to this scene. It speaks of God raising a storm and of how those on board ship 'trembled at the danger' but God 'hushed the storm to a murmur.'

who are well have no need of a physician, but those who are sick. Go and learn what this means, "I desire mercy, not sacrifice." For I have come to call not the righteous but sinners.'

Tax collectors were regarded as disloyal social outcasts because they collaborated with the imperial authorities, and were even suspected of treason because they collected taxes for the Romans. 'Sinners' was a technical term for members of despised trades thought susceptible to ritual uncleanness such as cameldrivers, sailors, herdsmen, shopkeepers, physicians, butchers etc. That Jesus would dine with such people was totally unacceptable to the Pharisees. But Jesus tells them that just as a physician must expose himself to the danger of contagious diseases, so, even if ritual uncleanness was a danger, he must mix with tax collectors and sinners to let them know that they too are beloved of God.

The disciples of John the Baptist come to Jesus, saying, 'Why do we and the Pharisees fast often, but your disciples do not fast?' Jesus answers them, 'The wedding guests cannot mourn as long as the bridegroom is with them, can they? The days will come when the bridegroom is taken away from them, and then they will fast.' Matthew understands fasting to be a sign of mourning. Jesus compares the disciples to wedding guests who rejoice while he, the bridegroom, is still with them. But after he leaves them, they will experience many tribulations, and therefore they will have good reasons for fasting.

Jesus then utters some rather the enigmatic words: 'No one sews a piece of un-shrunken cloth on an old cloak, for the patch pulls away from the cloak, and a worse tear is made. Neither is new wine put into old wineskins; otherwise, the skins burst, and the wine is spilled, and the skins are destroyed; but new wine is put into fresh wineskins, and so both are preserved.'

The old garment and the old wineskins stand for the Pharisees' interpretations of the Mosaic law. Jesus asserts, however, that something new and startling is now happening: the old, and good, law of Moses is being truly fulfilled in Jesus' teaching, as opposed to the teaching of the Pharisees, or even that of John the Baptist.

Finally Matthew tells us, Jesus goes around all the towns and villages, teaching in their synagogues, proclaiming the good news of the kingdom, and curing every disease and every sickness. When he sees the crowds, his heart is moved with pity for them because they are harassed and helpless, like sheep without a shepherd.[15] Then he says to his disciples, 'The harvest is plentiful, but the labourers are few; therefore ask the Lord of the harvest to send out labourers into his harvest.' Only faith, nourished through prayer, will generate more workers to carry on Christ's demanding mission.

---

15. Shepherd imagery is common throughout the Bible for political and religious leadership.

The Mission of the Apostles
(10:1-42)

Jesus summons the apostles and prepares to send them out on a mission, giving them authority over 'unclean spirits', and the power to cure every disease and sickness – the same powers that he exercises himself. Matthew names the twelve apostles: Simon, also known as Peter, and his brother Andrew; James son of Zebedee and his brother John; Philip and Bartholomew; Thomas and Matthew the tax collector; James son of Alphaeus, and Thaddaeus; Simon the Cannanaean, and Judas Iscariot, the one who betrays him.

The twelve names are slightly different in the other gospels,[1] but by placing Simon Peter first on the list, all the gospels recognise him as a spokesman for the group. The number twelve is significant in that it signifies the twelve tribes of Israel, the whole nation as it were, even though, by Jesus' time, the twelve tribes were no longer in existence. Symbolically the twelve apostles form the nucleus of the renewed Israel that is being formed around Jesus.

Jesus tells the twelve: 'Go nowhere among the Gentiles, and enter no town of the Samaritans, but go rather to the lost sheep of the house of Israel. As you go, proclaim the good news. "The kingdom of heaven has come near".' Jesus sees his own mission as being primarily to the people of Israel, although other statements in Matthew's gospel presume a mission to the Gentiles also. It is thought that many of the commissioning statements attributed to Jesus are in fact post-resurrection words of Christian prophets of the early church. For example, Jesus speaks about his disciples being 'led before governors and kings for my sake,

----

1. Mark 3:16-19; Luke 6;14-16; and Acts 1:13

to bear witness before them *and the pagans,*'[2] seemingly contradicting his statement about not going into pagan territory. Matthew's Jesus seems to be anticipating the kind of persecution by the Jewish authorities and by Gentiles that will greet the apostles only after the resurrection.

Jesus says, 'You received without payment; give without payment.' What Jesus teaches is so important for salvation that everyone must be taught without regard for people's ability to pay for the disciples' upkeep – even though 'labourers deserve their food.'

He tells the twelve that he is sending them out like sheep into the midst of wolves: 'So be wise as serpents and innocent as doves.' He warns them that they will be handed over to councils and flogged in synagogues, but that they are not to worry for 'What you are to say will be given to you at that time; for it is not you who speak, but the Spirit of your Father speaking through you.'

Families will be divided, Jesus warns them. 'Brother will betray brother to death, and a father his child, and children will rise against parents and have them put to death; and you will be hated by all on account of my name. But the one who endures to the end will be saved.' 'For truly, I tell you, you will not have gone through all the towns of Israel before the Son of Man comes.'

The persecuted disciples in one town are told to flee to the next. There was, in fact, no fierce, widespread, and possibly lethal persecution of Jesus' disciples by their fellow Israelites prior to Jesus' death. While Jesus anticipates his second coming as imminent, he leaves the time undetermined.

Jesus says: 'A disciple is not above the teacher, nor a slave above the master; it is enough for the disciple to be like the teacher, and the slave like the master. If they have called the master of the house[3] Be-el'zebul, how much more will they malign those of his household!' – Jesus' followers.

---

2. Matthew 10:18
3. Jesus himself

The word 'disciple' means student. Jesus is saying that his followers are to be his life-long students, because what he teaches them is wisdom about life itself. Unlike Jewish students who, having learned what the master has to teach, then move on from one master to another or become teachers themselves, Jesus' disciples are not to do this. For them, Jesus is to be the only teacher, as well as their abiding Lord.

Jesus urges his disciples not to fear those who kill the body but cannot kill the soul: 'Rather fear him who can destroy both body and soul in hell.'[4] Jesus, however, gives his disciples a word of encouragement: 'Are not two sparrows sold for a penny?' Sparrows were the cheapest food one could buy in the market. 'Yet not one of them will fall to the ground apart from your Father. And even the hairs of your head are counted.' He adds rather playfully, 'So do not be afraid; you are of more value than many sparrows.'

'Do not think that I have come to bring peace to the earth; I have not come to bring peace, but a sword. For I have come to set a man against his father, and a daughter against her mother, and a daughter-in-law against her mother-in-law; and one's foes will be members of one's own household.'

What are we to make of these strange words by the man who once said, 'Blessed are the peacemakers'? The sword is not to be understood as implying approval for some sort of uprising, but rather as a symbol for a very regrettable side effect of tension and division resulting from the uncompromising proclamation of God's kingdom, God's reign. Jesus is quoting the prophet Micah who spoke about widespread civil corruption and apostasy that leads to a breakdown of normal human and family relationships, where 'the son treats the father with contempt, the

---

4. Gehenna was the name of a rubbish dump just outside Jerusalem. Centuries before Jesus, the dump was well known as a place where children were burned alive as human sacrifices to pagan gods. As is the case with most rubbish dumps, it was a place where everything was being destroyed and/or being eaten by worms. The continuously smouldering fire completed the work of destruction and corruption. This was the origin of the Jewish and Christian image of hell.

daughter rises up against her mother, the daughter-in-law against her mother-in-law; your enemies are members of your own household.'[5]

Jesus goes on to say, 'Whoever loves father or mother more than me is not worthy of me; and whoever loves son or daughter more than me is not worthy of me; and whoever does not take up the cross and follow me is not worthy of me. Those who find their life will lose it, and those who lose their life for my sake will find it.'

To understand what Jesus means it is important to appreciate the fact that group solidarity was very important for the Jews. A family, tribe or nation was thought of as a kind of corporate personality. The basic unit was the family, and one's extended family included all one's relatives, who regarded each other as brothers, sisters, mothers and fathers. So all felt the harm done to any member of the family. The shame of one affected all: so one could say to an outsider, 'Whatever you do to the least of my brothers and sisters, you do to me.'[6]

Jesus sought a new kind of solidarity, one that excluded no one, not even one's enemies. It was not based simply on biological affinity but, much more radically, on doing the will of God. Jesus said, 'Who is my mother, and who are my brothers?' And pointing to his disciples, he said, 'Here are my mother and my brothers! For whoever does the will of my Father in heaven is my brother and sister and mother.'[7] This way of identifying his disciples as his new 'family' must really have shocked his listeners, not to mention members of his own biological and extended family. It would involve 'taking up the cross,' enduring great suffering, in order to follow him, and would even provoke family divisions. Following Jesus would involve 'losing' one's life, namely traditional Jewish solidarity, for Jesus' sake in order to find a more universal and life-giving solidarity with Jesus at its centre.

---

5. Micah 7:6
6. Matthew 25:40
7. Matthew 12:48-49

'Whoever welcomes you welcomes me', Jesus says to the twelve when he sends them out on their mission. 'And whoever welcomes me welcomes the one who sent me.' There was a legal principle governing any Jewish emissary: 'A man's agent is like himself.' So all who receive the disciples receive Jesus, and whoever receives Jesus receives the Father who sent him into the world. 'Whoever welcomes a prophet', a disciple who speaks in Jesus' name, 'will receive a prophet's reward; and whoever receives a righteous person will receive the reward of the righteous; and whoever gives a cup of cold water to one of these little ones in the name of a disciple – truly I tell you, none of these will lose their reward.' The 'little ones' are the Twelve Apostles. Later, Matthew suggests that 'little ones' was also a designation for members of his own community.[8]

---

8. Matthew 18:6, 10, 14

Opposition to Jesus
(11 and 12)

Matthew tells us that when John the Baptist was in prison he sent his disciples to Jesus to find out whether he was truly the Messiah. 'Are you the one who is to come, or are we to wait for another?' The reason for John's doubts was that Jesus' mission had not been one of fiery judgement that John had expected. Jesus answers them, quoting the prophet Isaiah, 'Go back and tell John what you hear and see: the blind see again and the lame walk, lepers are cleansed, and the deaf hear, and the dead are raised to life, and the good news is preached to the poor; and happy is the man who does not lose faith in me.'[1] This last beatitude was a warning to the Baptist and his followers not to disbelieve Jesus simply because he had not lived up to their own fiery expectations.

'Truly I tell you,' Jesus says, 'among those born of women, no one has arisen greater than John the Baptist; yet the least in the kingdom of heaven is greater then he.' To be part of God's rule, as proclaimed by Jesus, is so great a privilege that the person who is part of it is greater even than the Baptist. Jesus adds a strange saying: 'Since John the Baptist came, up to this present time, the kingdom has been subjected to violence, and the violent are taking it by storm.' The opponents of Jesus are trying to prevent people from accepting Jesus' teaching, or seek to undermine those who have already accepted it, even using force by expelling his followers from the synagogue.

So Jesus addresses them. 'To what will I compare this generation? It is like children sitting in the marketplaces and calling to one another, "We played the flute for you, and you did not dance; we wailed, and you did not mourn." For John came, nei-

---

1. Isaiah 29:18-19; 35:5-6; 61:1

ther eating nor drinking, and they say, "He has a demon"; the Son of Man came eating and drinking and they say, "Look, a glutton and a drunkard, a friend of tax collectors and sinners!" Yet wisdom is vindicated by her deeds.'

Like petulant children who will play none of the games suggested, the opponents of Jesus accept neither the stern lifestyle nor warnings of John the Baptist, nor the more gentle approach of Jesus. However the works (miracles) done by Jesus demonstrate that he embodies, and reveals, the wisdom of God.

Jesus then begins to reproach the towns where most of his mighty deeds have been done. 'Woe to you, Chorazin! Woe to Bethsaida!' two towns in upper Galilee. 'For if the deeds of power done in you had been done in Tyre and Sidon', (Gentile cities) 'they would have repented long ago in sackcloth and ashes. But I tell you on the day of judgement it will be more tolerable for Tyre and Sidon than for you.' Jesus' miracles are meant to provoke conversion among his fellow Jews, but in that they largely fail.

Jesus goes on to thank his Father for what has already been achieved. 'I thank you, Father, Lord of heaven and of earth, because you have hidden these things from the wise and intelligent,' (the scribes and Pharisees) 'and have revealed them to infants', those who do not count in this world. 'Yes, Father, for such was your gracious will. All things have been handed over to me by my Father.' Jesus can speak of the things of God because he is God's Son. 'No one knows the Son except the Father, and no one knows the Father except the Son and anyone to whom the Son chooses to reveal him.'[2]

'Come to me, all you who are weary and are carrying heavy burdens,' (those who were burdened by the Law as interpreted by the scribes and Pharisees) 'and I will give you rest (of soul). Take my yoke upon you, and learn from me; for I am gentle and humble in heart, and you will find rest for your souls. For my yoke is easy, and my burden is light.' The rabbis spoke of 'the yoke of Torah,' obedience to the teachings of the Law as they in-

---

2. To 'know' in the sense of being intimate with someone.

terpreted them. Jesus' yoke is easier because his teaching is shorter and centred simply on what is essential. But in many ways it is also more difficult, because the demands of love of God and neighbour are inexhaustible.

Conflict is mounting between Jesus and the Pharisees. His hungry disciples pick ears of grain on the Sabbath. The Pharisees object that what they have done is a breaking of the Sabbath. While the Old Testament gives a simple command to keep holy the Sabbath, the rabbis went on to classify thirty-nine kinds of work as forbidden, including reaping. Jesus counters the Pharisees' argument by citing the examples of King David and the temple priests and how they seemed to violate the law and yet were held to be innocent. Jesus then solemnly declares that, 'The Son of Man is lord of the Sabbath.' In other words, Jesus claims supreme authority over what Moses had pre-scribed. This must have shocked his Jewish listeners to the core. So, when Jesus cures a man with a withered hand on the Sabbath, it is understandable that the Pharisees conspire against him, and discuss how to destroy him.

When Jesus becomes aware of what the Pharisees are up to, he refuses to argue with them and instead leaves the area, and continues to cure people. He orders them 'not to make him known,' not to reveal to the Pharisees his true identity. Matthew quotes the prophet Isaiah to explain the sort of Messiah that Jesus is: one very different from normal Jewish expectations. 'Here is my servant, whom I have chosen, my beloved, with whom my soul is well pleased. I will put my spirit upon him, and he will proclaim justice to the Gentiles. He will not wrangle or cry aloud, nor will anyone hear his voice in the streets. He will not break a bruised reed or quench a smouldering wick until he brings justice to victory. And in his name the Gentiles will hope.'[3]

When Jesus cures a blind and mute person, the Pharisees claim that he does so by the power of Beelzebul, the prince of demons. Jesus claims, however, that it is by the Spirit of God

---

3. Isaiah 42:1-3

that he drives out demons. 'If it is by the Spirit of God that I cast out demons, then the kingdom of God has come to you.' 'I tell you, people will be forgiven for every sin and blasphemy, but blasphemy against the Spirit will not be forgiven. Whoever speaks a word against the Son of Man will be forgiven, but whoever speaks against the Holy Spirit will not be forgiven, either in this age or in the age to come.' Blasphemy against the Holy Spirit consists of obstinately attributing to the devil the power of God as it is manifested in Jesus' teaching and healing.

Addressing the Pharisees, Jesus says, 'Either make the tree good, and its fruit good; or make the tree bad, and its fruit bad; for the tree is known by its fruit.' His point is that the quality of a person is shown through one's deeds. That Jesus heals and cures shows that he is a good person. But the Pharisees are a 'brood of vipers!' 'How can you speak good things, when you are evil? For out of the abundance of the heart the mouth speaks.' Taking another swipe at the Pharisees, Jesus says, 'I tell you, on the day of judgement you will have to give an account for every careless word you utter; for by your words you will be justified, and by your words you will be condemned.' No wonder the Pharisees want to destroy Jesus!

Some of the scribes and Pharisees say to him, 'Teacher, we wish to see a sign from you.' They want some assurance or authentication that Jesus is truly from God. But he answers them, 'An evil and adulterous generation asks for a sign.' The term 'adulterous' is a metaphor describing Israel's infidelity. The assumption is that God's relationship to his people is like that between married couples. Jesus continues, 'No sign will be given to it except the sign of the prophet Jonah.[4] 'For just as Jonah was three days and three nights in the belly of the sea monster, so for three days and three nights will the Son of Man be in the heart of the earth.' Jesus' reference to his death is obvious. 'The people of Nineveh will rise up at the judgment with this generation and condemn it, because they repented at the proclamation of Jonah, and see, something greater than Jonah is here! The queen of the

---

4. Jonah chapter 3

South (the queen of Sheba)[5] will rise up in judgement with this generation and condemn it, because she came from the ends of the earth to listen to the wisdom of Solomon, and see, something greater than Solomon is here.' While the men of Nineveh were prepared to repent their evil ways, the Pharisees are not. Jesus' wisdom is greater than that of the wise king Solomon, but the scribes and Pharisees simply reject it.

Jesus now returns to the accusation by the Pharisees that he casts out demons by the power of the devil. 'When an unclean spirit goes out of a man it wanders through waterless country looking for a place to rest, and cannot find one. Then it says, "I will return to the home I came from." But on arrival, finding it unoccupied, swept and tidied, it then goes off and collects seven other spirits more evil than itself, and they go in and set up house there, so that the man ends up by being worse than he was before. This is what will happen to this evil generation.'

One is reminded of the alcoholic who gives up the 'demon' drink for a time, but then relapses, so that he ends up by being worse off than ever before. Jesus is a healer of troubled people. But evil can return if one does not fill the empty place left by the departed 'demon' with faith, hope and love. What applies to the individual person, applies even more to Jesus' generation because of their refusal to accept him as the Messiah. The situation that preceded his coming will now be made even worse because he has made known God's will, but people refuse to listen to him.

As Jesus addresses the crowd, he is told that his mother and brothers have arrived to speak to him. Jesus takes the opportunity to ask the crowd, including the scribes and Pharisees, a puzzling question, 'Who is my mother? Who are my brothers?' Without denying family ties, he asserts that anyone who does the will of the Father is his brother and sister and mother. The scribes and Pharisees, he implies, who refuse to listen to his voice simply have no part in the great family of those who carry out God's will.

5. 1 Kings 10:1-13

He Speaks in Parables
(13: 1-52)

Crowds gather round Jesus one day as he sits by the lakeside. So great is their number that he gets into a boat, while the people stand on the beach, and he tells them many things in parables, in stories, sayings, and even riddles. Jesus' stories are his way of explaining what he means when he speaks about the kingdom of heaven, God's reign. The dilemma for Matthew is this: why do some Jews accept Jesus while others do not? Jesus' parables are one way of answering this question.

'Listen', Jesus says, 'a sower went out to sow, and as he sowed, some seeds fell on the path, and the birds came and ate them up. Other seeds fell on rocky ground where they did not have much soil, and they sprang quickly, since they had no depth of earth. But when the sun rose, they were scorched; and, since they had no root, they withered away. Other seeds fell among thorns, and the thorns grew up and choked them. Other seeds feel on good soil and brought forth grain, some a hundredfold, some sixty, some thirty. Let anyone with ears listen!'

The disciples are puzzled as to why he speaks in parables. He replies, rather enigmatically, 'To you it has been given to know the secrets of the kingdom of heaven (the hidden plans, or designs of God), but to them (those who opposed Jesus' teaching, like the Pharisees) it has not been given. For to those who have, more will be given, and they will have an abundance: but from those who have nothing, even what they have will be taken away.' What Jesus means is that for those of good will, what they have learnt from the Jewish scriptures will be added to and perfected by what he teaches, but the ill-disposed will lose the perfection that he brings to the law of Moses.

Jesus goes on to say, 'The reason I speak to them in parables is that 'seeing they do not perceive, and hearing they do not listen, nor do they understand.' Jesus is quoting the prophet Isaiah, 'you will indeed listen, but never understand, and you will indeed look, but never perceive. For this people's heart has grown dull, and their ears are hard of hearing, and they have shut their eyes; so that they might not look with their eyes, and listen with their ears, and understand with their heart and turn.' Jesus is rebuking the Pharisees in particular but also all who bear him ill will, because 'they look and listen' but fail to truly hear and accept what the Jesus the prophet is saying.

However, Jesus praises the disciples. 'But blessed are your eyes, for they see, and your ears, for they hear. Truly I tell, many prophets and righteous people longed to see what you see, but did not see it, and to hear what you hear, but did not hear it.' Many people fail to understand Jesus' teaching, and so he uses his parables to make his point. He tells the disciples that they do see, do understand but, as the gospel will make clear later, their understanding is very limited indeed.

Jesus then explains the parable of the sower. 'When anyone hears the word of the kingdom and does not understand it, the evil one comes and snatches away what is sown in the heart: this is what was sown on the path. As for what was sown on rocky ground, this is the one who hears the word and immediately receives it with joy; yet such a person has no root, but endures only for a while, and when trouble or persecution arises on account of the word, that person immediately falls away. As for what was sown among thorns, this is the one who hears the word, but the cares of the world and the lure of wealth choke the word, and it produces nothing. But as for what was sown on good soil, this is the one who hears the word and understands it, who indeed bears fruit and yields, in one case a hundredfold, in another sixty, and in another thirty.' A superficial lifestyle, lack of endurance under stress and persecution, and the lure of wealth, make it extremely difficult for people to hear and understand God's word.

Another problem for the disciples, as for us, is why God allows good and evil to exist in the world. So Jesus tells them another parable. He compares the kingdom of heaven to a man who sows good seed in his field. An enemy comes and sows darnel, a type of grass that is found among cereal crops, and makes off: when the new wheat ripens so does the darnel. The owners' servants come to him and say, 'Master, did you not sow good seed in your field? Where, then, did these weeds come from?' The master answers, 'An enemy has done this.' The slaves say to him, 'Then do you want us to go and gather them?' But he replies, 'No; for in gathering in the weeds you would uproot the wheat along with them. Let both of them grow until the harvest; and at harvest time I will tell the reapers, Collect the weeds first and bind them in bundles to be burned, but gather the wheat into my barn.'

The 'harvest' Jesus speaks of is God's final judgement. The slaves are God's messengers. Yes, the disciples have to live in the world with people who are evil, but to destroy them could well involve destroying good people as well. The disciples have to be patient, tolerant and forbearing, until the future judgement by the Son of Man when there will be a separation of the just from the unjust.

Jesus then offers two other parables, one about a man, and the other about a woman, reflecting the even-handed way that Matthew deals with both sexes. He compares the kingdom of heaven to a mustard seed that someone plants in a field. 'It is the smallest of all the seeds, but when it has grown it is the greatest of shrubs and becomes a tree, so that the birds of the air come and make their nests in its branches.' Jesus is saying that the present small beginnings of the kingdom will experience extraordinary growth.

'The kingdom of heaven is like yeast that a woman took and mixed in with three measures of flour until all of it was leavened.' The sight of dough rising, due to the effect of the yeast, is used by Jesus to point to the surprising effect a small movement can have on the whole of society. God's plan, working almost invisibly, achieves great things as the kingdom grows.

'The kingdom of heaven is like treasure hidden in a field, which someone found and hid; then in his joy he goes and sells all that he has and buys that field. Again, the kingdom of heaven is like a merchant in search of fine pearls; on finding one pearl of great value, he went and sold all he that he had and bought it.' In Jesus' day, the political conditions in Palestine, with the continuing threat of invasion, were such that the burial of one's valuables was a common way of protecting them. Jesus is saying that God's reign is such a priceless treasure that a wise person would gladly give all for a chance to be part of it; it is the chance of a lifetime!

Jesus tells a parable about a net that is cast into the sea bringing in a haul of good fish and bad. The fishermen put the good into baskets but throw out the bad. 'So it will be at the end of the age. The angels will come out and separate the evil from the righteous and throw them into the furnace of fire, where there will be weeping and gnashing of teeth.' The kingdom is a mixed body of saints and sinners. The final sorting out must be left to God and his angelic agents.

Jesus asks, 'Have you understood all this?' They answer yes, but one has to wonder. 'Therefore every scribe who has been trained for the kingdom of heaven is like the master of a household who brings out of his treasure what is new and what is old.' Perhaps the author of the gospel sees himself as such a scribe. Scribes were originally charged with drawing up legal documents and interpreting the Torah. The point of the saying is that the old treasure, the Jewish heritage, and the new, what Jesus says and does, are to be valued. After all, Jesus did not come to abolish the law, but to bring it to perfection.

Finally, Jesus comes to his hometown of Nazareth, presumably where his family and neighbours live. He begins to teach the people in their synagogue in such a way that they are amazed and astounded. They say, 'Where did this man get this wisdom and these deeds of power?' Their question refers to Jesus' activities as a teacher and healer. Is his wisdom and healing ability from God or from the evil one, they wonder. By way of dismissal they say, 'Is not this the carpenter's son? Is his mother not called Mary? Are not his brothers James and Joseph and Simon and Judas? And are not his all his sisters with us? Where did this man get all this?' And they take offence at him, and so turn their anger and opposition against him. Because the people of Nazareth know about Jesus' family and presumably knew him from the past, they assume that they know all about him. They fail to understand that the source of his wisdom and mighty deeds is God.

Jesus says to them, 'Prophets are not without honour except in their own country and in their own house.' Jesus' comment has the ring of a popular proverb. As one author puts it, this whole text is an example of the 'prejudice of familiarity'. His neighbours assume they know all there is to know about Jesus, and so they dismiss him. Such a reaction is not uncommon even in today's world: in offices, schools, churches, and families. One can only imagine the hurt that Jesus must have experienced in his own hometown.

Feeding the Multitude
(14:1-15:39)

Herod has heard reports about Jesus. He thinks that Jesus is John the Baptist come back from the dead. Herod had arrested John, and put him in prison on account of Herodias, his brother Philip's wife, whom he had married, because John had been telling him, 'It is not lawful for you to have her.' Though Herod wanted to put him to death, he feared the crowd, because they regarded John as a prophet.

When Herod's birthday comes around, the daughter of Herodias dances before the invited guests, and she pleases Herod so much that he promises on oath to grant her whatever she might ask. Prompted by her mother, she asks for the head of John the Baptist on a platter. Herod is grieved, yet because of his oaths before the guests, he commands it to be given. John is beheaded, and his head is brought to Herodias by her daughter.[1]

After John's execution, John's disciples come and take the body and bury it; then they go and tell Jesus. He immediately takes a boat, and goes to a deserted place by himself. But when the crowds that had been following him hear this, they follow him on foot from the towns. Jesus goes ashore and, seeing the crowd, he has compassion for them, and cures their sick.

When time for the evening meal comes around, the disciples come and say to Jesus, 'This is a deserted place, and the hour is now late; send the crowds away so that they may go into the villages and buy some food for themselves.' Jesus says to them,

---

The Jewish historian Josephus has a different version of this story. According to him, Herod had become alarmed at John's popularity, and was afraid that he and his disciples might engage in some sort of rebellion. This, according to Josephus, is why Herod has him put to death.

'They need not go away; you give them something to eat.' They reply, 'We have nothing here but five loaves and two fish.' Jesus says, 'Bring them here to me,' and he orders the crowd to sit down on the grass. Taking the five loaves and two fish, he looks up to heaven, blesses and breaks the loaves, and gives them to the disciples who, in turn, give them to the crowds. Having had their fill, they collect what is left over of the broken pieces, twelve baskets full. Those who had eaten numbered about five thousand, besides women and children.

The story of Jesus feeding five thousand men, to say nothing of women and children, is to be found in various versions in all four gospels, and the next story of Jesus walking on the water is linked to it in the gospels of Matthew, Mark and John.[2] This suggests that both stories came from a very old tradition but underwent many adaptations during the early preaching of the gospel. Matthew even has another version of the story in chapter fifteen.[3]

On the obvious level, the story of the feeding of the five thousand represents Jesus' divine power put to the service of a hungry multitude whose predicament touches his heart. However there are echoes that hark back to the Old Testament. The feeding story harks back to the prophet Elisha feeding one hundred people with loaves, or even to the miracle of the manna given to the Israelites in the desert in Moses' time.[4]

The story of the feeding of the multitude also looks forward to the Last Supper where Jesus 'took some bread, said the blessing, broke it and gave it to his disciples.'[5] For Matthew, the crowds in the story represent the new Israel gathered around Jesus, while the twelve baskets represent the twelve tribes of Israel, the whole people gathered around the twelve apostles.

Directly after the feeding of the five thousand, Matthew tells us, Jesus makes his disciples get into a boat and go on ahead to

2. Matthew 14:13- 33; Mark 6:31-44; Luke 9:10-17; John 6:1-13
3. Matthew 15:32-39
4. See 11 Kings 4:42- 44 and Exodus 16:4 -35
5. Matthew 26:26

the other side, while he sends the crowds away. Then he goes into the hill country by himself to pray. When evening comes, he is there alone, while the boat, by now far out on the lake, is battling with a heavy sea, for there is a head-wind.

In the 'fourth watch' of the night, between three and six in the morning, Jesus goes towards them, walking on the lake and, when they see him, they are terrified. 'It is a ghost,' they say, and they cry out in fear. But at once Jesus calls out to them saying, 'Courage! It is I. Do not be afraid.' Peter answers, 'Lord, if it is you, tell me to come to you across the water.' 'Come,' says Jesus. Then Peter gets out of the boat and starts walking towards Jesus across the water, but as soon as he feels the force of the wind, he takes fright and begins to sink. 'Lord, save me!' he cries. Jesus puts out his hand at once and holds him. 'Man of little faith,' he says, 'why did you doubt?' And as they get into the boat the wind drops. The men in the boat bow down before him and say to Jesus, 'Truly, you are the Son of God.'

In this story we again find many echoes of the Old Testament. The divine identity of Jesus is stressed by what he says to the disciples, 'Courage, it is I' or literally 'I am.' In the book of Exodus, God is asked by what name he wants to be known when Moses addresses the Israelites, God answers, 'Thus you shall say to the Israelites, "I Am has sent me to you".'[6] Psalm 107 says, 'They cried aloud to the Lord in their trouble, and he brought them out of their distress; he made the storm be still, and the waves of the sea were hushed.'[7] The book of Job refers to God, saying, 'He alone stretched out the heavens and trampled the waves of the sea.'[8]

Peter's actions are a combination of impulsive love and faith weakened by doubt. Any man of faith would sink unless the Lord saved him. So Peter represents all those disciples who have faith in Jesus as the Son of God, but often doubt, yet gain strength from his powerful, helping hand.

---

6. Exodus 3:14
7. Psalm 107:28-29
8. Job 9:8

Later Christians too, while often sharing the same love and doubt, would find their strength in Christ's abiding presence in the Eucharist. For a small church struggling in a hostile world and feeling bereft of Jesus' presence, Jesus walking on the waters symbolises Jesus revealing himself as divine, coming to a small group of believers labouring in the night of a hostile, stormy world, but giving them courage, and calming their fears, especially through their celebration of the Eucharist. The story is a parable of the young church, the bark of Peter, besieged, vulnerable, and stepping out into the unknown.

Jesus now arrives in Gennesaret, on the western shore of the Sea of Galilee. People recognise him, and sending word throughout the region, they bring all who are sick, and beg him that they might touch even the fringe of his cloak, and all who touch it are healed. The 'fringe' probably refers to the tassels worn by pious Jews as a reminder to keep God's commandments.

Some Pharisees and scribes arrive from Jerusalem to challenge Jesus. For Matthew, it is the Pharisees, even more than the scribes or Sadducees, who are the adversaries of Jesus during his public ministry. He quotes Jesus as saying, 'Watch out, and beware of the yeast of the Pharisees and Sadducees.'[9] This 'yeast' describes an evil influence that can spread like an infection.

Matthew tells us that Pharisees and scribes from Jerusalem come to Jesus and say, 'Why do your disciples break the traditions of the elders? For they do not wash their hands before they eat?' Jesus answers them, 'And why do you break away from the commandment of God for the sake of your tradition? For God said, "Honour your father and your mother," and "Whoever speaks evil of father and mother must surely die." But you say, "Whoever tells father and mother whatever support you might have had from me is given to God," then that person need not honour the father. So for the sake of your tradition, you make void the word of God. You hypocrites! Isaiah prophesised right about you, "This people honour me with their lips, but their

---

9. Matthew 16:6

hearts are far from me; in vain do they worship me, teaching human precepts as doctrines".'[10]

Jesus then calls the people to him and says, 'Listen and understand: it is not what goes into the mouth that defiles the person, but it is what comes out of the mouth that defiles.' The disciples tell Jesus that the Pharisees had taken offence at what he had said, but as far as Jesus in concerned they are merely blind guides leading the blind.

When Peter asks Jesus for an explanation of what he means, he says, 'What comes out of the mouth proceeds from the heart,[11] and is what defiles. For out of the heart come evil intentions, murder, adultery, fornication, theft, false witness, slander. These are what defile a person, but to eat with unwashed hands does not defile.' As far as Jesus was concerned, eating with unwashed hands does not make someone ritually impure.

The teaching of the Pharisees fails to feed the multitude, whereas his teaching and actions do. So Jesus moves on to where his ministry will prove more fruitful. He goes towards Tyre and Sidon on the Mediterranean coast, traditionally regarded as a pagan area northwest of Jewish territory. There a Canaanite woman from the region comes out shouting, 'Have mercy on me, Lord, Son of David; my daughter is tormented by a demon.' He does not answer her. The disciples urge him to send her away 'for she keeps shouting after us'. He answers, 'I was sent only to the lost sheep of the house of Israel.' But the woman comes and kneels before him, saying, 'Lord, help me.' He answers her, 'It is not fair to take the children's food and throw it to the dogs.' She replies, 'Yes, Lord, yet even the dogs eat the crumbs that fall from their master's table.' Then Jesus answers her, 'Woman, great is your faith! Let it be done for you as you wish.' And the woman's daughter is healed instantly. Jesus affirms the traditional Jewish approach that salvation is for the Jews in the first instance, and then for the Gentiles. This incident

---

10. Isaiah 29:13
11. For the Jews the heart was the place of human understanding and human feeling.

would have appealed to Matthew's community, given its emphasis on Jesus' Jewish roots but also its mission to the Gentiles.

Matthew then tells the story of the feeding of the four thousand which is very similar to what we have seen in the feeding of the five thousand. Apart from the difference in numbers, the two stories are broadly similar. Jesus takes seven loaves and the few small fish that the disciples have in their possession; and after giving thanks, breaks them and gives them to the disciples to distribute to the assembled crowd. After all have eaten, the disciples take up the broken pieces left over, seven baskets full.

Matthew is again hinting at the future Eucharistic celebrations of his own community. He stresses the role of the disciples in the distribution of the bread, reflecting the role of ministers in his community. The mention of 'four thousand men, besides women and children' also hints at the multitude who will receive the Eucharistic bread, Gentiles as well as Jews.

Controversies
(16:1-28)

In Jesus' day there existed various groups or factions vying for influence in Israel. It is worth looking briefly at some of those mentioned by Matthew in his gospel. The Pharisees were a religious-political group of devout Jews who enjoyed a reputation for their precise interpretation of the Mosaic Law. The Pharisees admitted openly that some of their legal views and practices were not to be found in the written Mosaic law, but they insisted that such practices were venerable 'traditions' handed down by the 'fathers' or the 'elders' and that such practices were part of God's will for all of Israel. Jesus would refute this contention.

The Scribes were teachers, able to write texts and learned in the Mosaic law. They enjoyed authority and prestige within Jewish society. Mark's gospel speaks of 'the scribes of the Pharisees.'[1] They were, in effect, professional scribes who belonged to and were teachers in the party of the Pharisees.

The Sadducees were a religious-political group drawn mainly from among aristocratic laymen and members of the high-priestly families. Generally speaking they lacked a following among the common people. They rejected some of the beliefs favoured by the Pharisees, most notably belief in the resurrection of the dead, as well as the 'traditions handed down by the elders'. For Matthew it is the Pharisees, even more than the scribes or Sadducees, who are the adversaries of Jesus.

Matthew tells us that Pharisees and Sadducees come from Jerusalem and ask Jesus for 'a sign from heaven'. They want Jesus to produce some spectacular display that will show that he is from God. But he simply points to the sky: 'When it is evening, you say, "It will be fair weather, for the sky is red." And in the

---

1. Mark2:16

morning, "It will be stormy today, for the sky is red and threat-ening." You know how to interpret the appearance of the sky, but you cannot interpret the signs of the times.' Interpreting the signs of the times means being attentive to God's word in each generation. Jesus then adds, 'An evil and adulterous generation asks for a sign, but no sign will be given to it except the sign of Jonah.' It is an 'adulterous generation' because Israel's leaders are unfaithful to God. Jonah's 'sign' was his call to repentance made to the citizens of Nineveh. In the same way, Jesus calls the Pharisees and Sadducees to repentance.

When the disciples reach the other side of the Sea of Galilee, they find that they have forgotten to bring any bread. Jesus says to them, 'Watch out, and beware of the yeast of the Pharisees and Sadducees.' However, the disciples misunderstand him. 'Is it because we have brought no bread?' they ask one another. One can hear Jesus' exasperation. 'You of little faith, why are you talking about having no bread. Do you still not perceive?' He reminds them of the feedings of the five and four thousands.[2] 'Do you still not perceive? Do you not remember the five loaves for the five thousand, and how many baskets you gathered? How could you fail to perceive that I was not speak-ing about bread? Beware of the yeast of the Pharisees and Sadducees!' Just as yeast ferments dough, but can also make it go bad, so the perverse teachings of the Pharisees spread like an infection and misguide those for whom they are responsible. The disciples understand that Jesus is talking about the Pharisees' and Sadducees' teaching.

When they arrive at Caesarea Philippi, a town to the north of the Sea of Galilee, Jesus asks them, 'Who do people say that the Son of Man is?'[3] They answer, 'Some say John the Baptist, but others Elijah, and still others Jeremiah or one of the prophets.' Jeremiah is mentioned because he, like Jesus, was a prophet who

---

2. Matthew 14: 13ff and15:32ff
3. Matthew has inherited the Son of Man title from the prophet Daniel, who, in one of his visions, refers to one like 'a son of man' coming with the clouds of heaven.' (7:13)

experienced rejection and suffering. Jesus then asks, 'But who do you say I am?' Simon Peter answers him, 'You are the Messiah, the Son of the living God.' Matthew has added, 'Son of the living God' to direct attention away from any military-nationalistic connotations the title 'messiah' might have for the disciples.

Jesus answers Peter, 'Blessed are you, Simon son of Jonah! For flesh and blood has not revealed this to you, but my Father in heaven. And I tell you, you are Peter, and on this rock I will build my church, and the gates of Hades[4] will not prevail against it. I will give you the keys of the kingdom of heaven, and whatsoever you bind on earth will be bound in heaven, and whatever you loose on earth will be loosed in heaven.'

By the time the gospel came to be written, Matthew's church was already a structured group, a gathering of followers of Jesus. To be a church, a community of disciples, was the way in which the teaching and memory of Jesus was preserved. For Matthew, the pre-eminent disciple was Peter whose name in Greek was *Petros*, perhaps a nickname, a sort of play on words, given him by Jesus since the Greek work for rock was *petra*.

The meaning of Peter's ability to 'bind and loose' is debated by scholars, but the most likely interpretation is that Peter is being given the power to teach what must be observed by church members, with the result that Peter becomes, as it were, the chief rabbi of the Christian assembly. Binding and loosing were technical terms used by the rabbis that could refer either to binding the devil through exorcism, or to the juridical act of ex-communication. Jesus' words, coming as they do after a warning against the teaching of the Pharisees and the Sadducees, appear to support the latter interpretation.

'You are Peter' is one of the most discussed passages in the New Testament because Catholics have used it in support of the papacy. In the early Christian view, Jesus was a successor to John the Baptist, and this may have facilitated the idea that

---

4. Hades, or Sheol, refers to a general dwelling place of souls after death.

Jesus' principal disciple, Peter, would be his successor. Given the New Testament evidence about the role of Peter, it is not easy for those who reject the papacy to portray the concept of a successor to Peter as contradictory to the gospels.

Jesus sternly orders his disciples not to tell anyone that he is the Messiah, again to make sure that he is not seen as a military-nationalistic type figure. Indeed what follows in Mathew's gospel clearly demonstrates that Jesus is a very different messiah from the one most Jews expect. According to Matthew, 'Jesus began to show his disciples that he must go to Jerusalem and undergo great sufferings at the hands of the elders, chief priests and scribes, and be killed, and on the third day be raised.' Peter takes him aside and rebukes him, saying, 'God forbid it, Lord!' But Jesus turns and says to Peter, 'Get behind me, Satan! You are a stumbling block for me; for you are setting your mind not on divine things but on human things.'

It is unlikely that Jesus spoke in such precise terms about his fate. Matthew's words are probably a prophecy after the fact. That Jesus refers to Peter as Satan is another way of indicating that what Peter is saying is a form of temptation. Calling Peter 'a stumbling block' is an ironic reference to the fact that, a few moments before, he had said that Peter was to be 'the rock' on which the church was to be built.

That Jesus is no military-nationalistic messiah is confirmed again when he says, 'If any want to become my followers, let them deny themselves and take up their cross and follow me.' Self-denial means submission of oneself to God's will. Taking up one's cross is not a reference to Jesus' crucifixion, though Matthew's readers must surely have that in mind. This terrible death was common in Jesus' time, and taking up one's cross was a proverbial way of speaking about harsh suffering.

'For those who want to save their life will lose it, and those who lose their life for my sake will find it.' Those who want to save their lives, the deep inner core of their spiritual selves, are those who want to avoid martyrdom. Those who lose their lives, for Jesus' sake will, paradoxically, find eternal life. 'For what will it profit them if they gain the whole world but forfeit their life? Or what will they give in return for their life?' All the wealth in the world will not lead to happiness which can only be found in carrying out God's will. Then referring to what will happen at the end of the world, Jesus says, 'For the Son of Man is to come with his angels in the glory of his Father, and then he will repay everyone for what has been done.'[5]

'Truly I tell you, there are some standing here who will not taste death before they see the Son of Man coming in his kingdom.' Since the coming of God's kingdom in all its fullness has yet to take place, the most obvious reference to those 'who will not see death' is a reference to what takes place at the Transfiguration.

5. A reference to Psalm 62:12. 'For you, (Lord), repay to all according to their work.'

The Transfiguration
(17:1-27)

Jesus takes Peter, James and his brother John, and leads them up a high mountain by themselves. He is transfigured before them, and his face shines like the sun, and his clothes become dazzling white. Suddenly there appear Moses and Elijah, talking with him. Peter says to Jesus. 'Lord, it is good for us to be here; if you wish, I will make three booths here, one for you, one for Moses, and one for Elijah.' While he is still speaking, a bright cloud suddenly overshadows them, and from the cloud a voice says, 'This is my Son, the Beloved; with him I am well pleased; listen to him.' When the disciples hear this, they fall to the ground and are overcome by fear. But Jesus comes and touches them, saying, 'Get up and do not be afraid.' And when they look up, they see no one except Jesus alone.

What are we to make of this remarkable scene? The words of Jesus to his disciples that precede this scene can help us understand what it is all about. 'Truly I tell you there are some standing here who will not taste death before they see the Son of Man coming in his kingdom.' Jesus, like John the Baptist before him, proclaims the imminent coming of God's full reign, but clearly that moment does not arrive in Jesus' lifetime

However, the Transfiguration can be seen as a partial fulfilment of his promise that some would not die before Jesus comes in his kingdom. Given that Jesus speaks of what has happened as 'a vision', it has been surmised that the story may have been a vision accorded to Peter, perhaps after the resurrection, during the Jewish feast of Tabernacles (or Booths), in which he received further insight into who Jesus really was. So the story may be an externalisation of some inner spiritual experience that Peter, James and John shared.

Like so many stories in the gospels, the Transfiguration story is full of allusions to the Old Testament. Jesus going up a high mountain recalls the story of God speaking to Moses on Mount Sinai.[1] We are told that Jesus' face shone like the sun, just as Moses' face did because he had been talking to God, and that Jesus' clothes 'became dazzling white'. Jesus becomes a being of light; his nature becomes luminous, transparent to the disciples' gaze. Peter's role is central to the story. He suggests making three booths (the Israelites once had a practice of living in booths in the fields during harvest time): one for the great lawgiver Moses, one for the great prophet Elijah, and one for Jesus. Suddenly a bright cloud covers them all. The cloud represents the divine presence, the cloud of unknowing, in which God is met and heard. A voice from the cloud speaks, 'This is my Son, the Beloved; with him I am well pleased; listen to him!' The voice from God uses the same words that were used at Jesus' baptism.[2] The disciples fall on their faces in fear at the sound of God's voice but Jesus comes up and touches them. When the disciples look up they see no one, only Jesus. Moses and Elijah have withdrawn. The story suggests that Moses and Elijah have diminished in significance now that the full revelation of God has come in the person of Jesus.

As they come down from the mountain, Jesus says, 'Tell no one about the vision until the Son of Man has been raised from the dead.' And the disciples ask him, 'Why, then, do the scribes say then that Elijah has to come first?'[3] 'True', he replies, 'Elijah is indeed coming and will restore all things; but I tell you that Elijah has already come, and they did not recognise him, but did to him whatever they pleased. So also the Son of Man is about to suffer at their hands.' The disciples understand that he has been speaking of John the Baptist.

Peter has already confessed that Jesus is the Messiah. When

---

1. Exodus 34:1-35
2. Matthew 3:17
3. According to the prophet Malachi the return of the prophet Elijah will precede the coming of the Day of the Lord. (4:5-6)

Jesus had asked, 'Who do people say the Son of Man is?' Peter had replied, 'You are the Christ (the Messiah), the Son of the living God.'[4] During the Transfiguration vision Peter, James and John see a further manifestation of the divine presence, but they are surprised that Elijah has not played the part assigned to him by the scribes. However, Jesus replies that Elijah has, in fact, performed that function, though unrecognised, in the person of John the Baptist. Hence, because the disciples have seen and acknowledged that Jesus is of divine origin, he was able to say to them 'There are some standing here who will not taste death before they see the Son of Man coming in his kingdom.' God's kingdom is being inaugurated by what Jesus says and does.

Matthew goes on to give us another example of Jesus inaugurating God's kingdom. A man comes to him, kneels before him and says, 'Lord, have mercy on my son, for he is an epileptic and he suffers terribly; he often falls into the fire and often into the water. And I brought him to your disciples, but they could not cure him.'

Jesus turns on the disciples and, in an exasperated tone, says, 'You faithless and perverse generation, how much longer must I be with you? How much longer must I put up with you?' He then says, 'Bring him here to me.' Jesus rebukes the son's 'demon', and the boy is cured instantly. Later, the disciples come privately to Jesus, and ask why they were unable to cure the boy. 'Because of your little faith', he tells them. 'For truly I tell you, if you have faith the size of a mustard seed, you will say to this mountain, 'Move from here to there,' and it will move; and nothing will be impossible for you.'

The mustard seed and the moving of mountains are both metaphors. Faith, *like* a mustard seed, is an apparently small and insignificant thing that can achieve the impossible, *like* moving mountains. The faith Jesus speaks of is not the same as subscribing to creeds or doctrines and dogmas. It is the conviction that God is good to humanity and that God's power of goodness and truth can and will triumph over all evil.

---

4. Matthew 16:16-17

As they gather in Galilee, Jesus tells them, 'The Son of Man is going to be betrayed into human hands, and they will kill him, and on the third day he will be raised.' And the disciples are greatly distressed. Is this another post-factum prophecy inserted by Matthew?

When they reach Capernaum, the collectors of the temple tax[5] come to Peter and ask, 'Does your teacher not pay the temple tax?' Peter says that he does. When Peter comes home, Jesus asks him, 'What do think, Simon? From whom do kings of the earth take toll or tribute? From their children or from others?' Peter says, 'From others.' Jesus says, 'Then the children are free. However, so that we do not give offence to them, go to the sea and cast a hook; take the first fish that comes up; and when you open its mouth, you will find a coin; take that and give it to them for you and me.'

Strictly speaking no miracle is involved here. Matthew never tells us that Peter actually caught the fiscally philanthropic fish! The story of the fish is probably a folkloric addendum by Matthew. The point of the story is that kings or rulers do not pay taxes: other people pay taxes to them. So Jesus, as Son of God, and his disciples are exempt from paying the temple tax but, in order not to give scandal to their fellow Jews, and to demonstrate to the Romans that they are peaceful citizens, they agree to pay it on a voluntary basis. As Jesus says, 'Give to the emperor the things that are the emperor's, and to God the things that are God's.'[6]

---

5. Since Matthew was writing after the destruction of the Jerusalem Temple in AD70, the temple tax mentioned here may well have been the punitive two denarii tax imposed on Jews to support the temple of Jupiter Capitolinus in Rome. Such contributions to pagan worship would have been highly offensive to Jews and Christians alike.
6. Matthew 22:21

True Greatness
(18:1-35)

The disciples come to Jesus and ask, 'Who is the greatest in the kingdom of heaven?' The disciples' question is very appropriate in a society in which social status was taken very seriously. So Jesus calls a young child to him, and sets him in front of the disciples. 'Truly I tell you, unless you change and become like children, you will never enter the kingdom of heaven. Whoever becomes humble like this child is the greatest in the kingdom of heaven.' In Jesus' set of values the humble are more important than the powerful because they tend to depend on God more than those who are rich. Jesus' remark about becoming like young children challenges the disciples' assumptions about social status because children had no status and no social importance.

'Whoever welcomes one such child in my name welcomes me. If any of you put a stumbling block before one of these little ones, it would be better for you if a great millstone were fastened around your neck and you were drowned in the depth of the sea. Woe to the world because of stumbling blocks! Occasions for stumbling are bound to come, but woe to the one by whom the stumbling block comes!' Why must there be obstacles? Because God has created people with the capacity for moral struggle and mutual influence, so they can use that freedom to sin and to exploit others.

Using deliberately exaggerated language, Jesus says, 'If your hand or your foot causes you to stumble, cut it off and throw it away; it is better for you to enter into life maimed, than to have two hands or two feet and to be thrown into the eternal fire. And if your eye should cause you to stumble, tear it out and throw it away; it is better for you to enter life with one eye than to have two eyes and to be thrown into the hell of fire.'[1] The condemnation of scandals that can cause believers to turn away from God was very appropriate for Matthew's church, if one is to judge by the disputes that went on in the churches founded by St Paul.[2]

Matthew's basic concern was with life *within* the Christian community. This is why he addresses problems of status-seeking, scandal, and straying members as Jesus' next words demonstrate.

'Take care that you do not despise one of these little ones; for I tell you, in heaven their angels continually see the face of my Father in heaven.[3] What do you think? If a shepherd had a hundred sheep, and one of them has gone astray, does he not leave the ninety-nine on the mountains and go in search of the one that went astray? And if he finds it, truly I tell you, he rejoices over it more than over the ninety-nine that never went astray. So it is not the will of your Father in heaven that one of these little ones should be lost.' The 'little ones' referred to here are community members who stray from the Christian community.[4]

By most worldly standards organisations are successful to the extent that they take care of the majority. A political leader, for example, who could retain ninety-nine percent of his constituency, would have the most favourable poll ratings in history. It would seem better to let one person perish than to have the whole institution destroyed. Jesus, however, has a different set of values that he expresses in ways that often look impractical but that catch his outlook. No large church (or no large parish) could follow what he suggests as a regular practice, for the ninety-nine per cent of those who had not strayed would revolt at being neglected. Nevertheless Jesus' values must not be forgotten; for

---

1. The reference is to Gehinnom, a valley in Jerusalem that was once polluted by infant sacrifice.
2. cf 1 Corinthians 8:13; 11:19
3. The guardian angels of the 'little ones' were said to have unrestricted access to the divine presence. cf Acts 12:15
4. In Ezekiel the shepherds of Israel, the leaders, are criticised by God: 'I will seek the lost, and I will bring back the strayed, and I will bind up the injured, and I will strengthen the weak, but the fat and strong I will destroy. I will feed them with justice.' (34:16)

when they are put into practice, however seldom, at that moment and in that place God's kingdom becomes a reality. Jesus calls into question our ideas about social status and personal importance. It is sobering to note that the church in the first century had much the same problems that face Christians today.

'If another member of the church[5] sins against you, go and point out the fault when the two of you are alone. If the member listens to you, you have regained that one. But if you are not listened to, take one or two others along with you, so that every word may be confirmed by the evidence of two or three witnesses. If the member refuses to listen to them, tell it to the church; and if the offender refuses to listen even to the church, let such a one be to you as a Gentile and a tax collector.' The three-step procedure for reconciling a church member probably reflects the practice in Matthew's community. The expression 'as a Gentile and a tax collector' presupposes a largely Jewish audience who tended to look down on such people. Earlier in Matthew's gospel Gentiles and tax collectors demonstrate great faith in Jesus.[6]

'Truly, I tell you, whatever you bind on earth will be bound in heaven, and whatever you loose on earth will be loosed in heaven. Again, truly I tell you if two of you agree on earth about anything you ask, it will be done for you by my Father in heaven. For where two or three are gathered in my name, I am there among them.' God stands behind community decisions, and Jesus lives within the community gathered in his name, that is to say seeking to carry on his mission.

The power to bind and loose, previously bestowed on Peter,[7] is now given to the disciples. What is being given is the power to either impose or lift excommunication from the community, or forgive, or not forgive, sins. The context of 'where two or three are gathered' is judicial and not primarily liturgical. It reflects rabbinic teaching: 'If two sit together and words of the law pass between them, the divine presence abides between them.'

5. The local congregation
6. Matthew 8:5-13: 9:9-13: 11:19: 15:21-28
7. Matthew 16:19

Peter then asks Jesus about how often he must forgive anyone who wrongs him. Is it to be seven times? Jesus replies, 'Not seven times, but, I tell you, seventy-seven times,' or, in other words, an infinite number of times. There must be no limits to the willingness to forgive. To illustrate his point, Jesus relates a parable about an unforgiving servant that illustrates what he means about forgiveness without limits.

A slave owed a king ten thousand talents, an astronomical sum (like a billion euro for us) which the slave could never repay. Since he cannot pay that sum, the king orders him to be sold, together with his wife and children and all his possessions, and payment of the debt be made. Such a practice did not exist in Jesus' time, so we have to conclude that the king was a Gentile, and what he commanded was intended as an act of punishment. The slave falls on his knees before the king, asking for patience, and he says that he will repay the debt. Out of pity, the king releases him and forgives him his debt.

This same slave then encounters one of his fellow slaves who owes him a hundred denarii, equivalent to a hundred days wages. He seizes him by the throat and says, 'Pay what you owe.' His fellow slave pleads with him in the same words that he had used, 'Have patience with me, and I will pay you.' But he refuses and has him thrown into prison until such time as he can pay the debt. When the other slaves see what has happened, they go to the king and report all that had taken place. The king summons him and says, 'You wicked slave! I forgave you all that debt because you pleaded with me. Should you not have had mercy on your fellow slave as I had mercy on you?' In anger, he hands the slave over to be tortured until he would pay his entire debt.

Jesus says to his disciples, 'So my heavenly Father will also do to every one of you, if you do not forgive your brother or sister from your heart.' In other words, if you want mercy from God, be merciful to others. If you exact justice from others, expect the same from God. As Jesus put it, 'If you forgive others their trespasses, your heavenly Father will also forgive you; but if you do not forgive others, neither will your Father forgive your trespasses.'[8]

All that Jesus has to say has real application today, especially for the many who turn away from the church because they do not find ready forgiveness. To the extent that churches listen to what Jesus has to say, they keep his spirit alive.

---

8. Matthew 6:14

On the Road to Jerusalem
(19 and 20)

As Jesus begins his journey to Jerusalem, where suffering and death await him, he gives the disciples instructions about how they should behave as leaders of his community of disciples. First, however, there is an encounter with the Pharisees. They approach Jesus and ask him, 'Is it lawful for a man to divorce his wife for any cause?' Jesus, quoting the book of Genesis,[1] answers, 'Have you not read that the one who made them at the beginning "made them male and female," and says, "For this reason a man shall leave his father and mother and be joined to his wife, and the two shall become one flesh." Therefore what God has joined together, let no one separate.'

The Pharisees reply, 'Why then did Moses command us to give a certificate of dismissal and to divorce her?' Jesus replies, 'It was because you were so hard-hearted that Moses allowed you to divorce your wives, but from the beginning it was not so. And I say to you, whoever divorces his wife, except for un-chastity, and marries another commits adultery.'

What does Jesus mean when he says that divorce is not permissible *except for un-chastity*, or, as some translations have it, fornication? Some people interpret the exception as meaning that where one partner commits adultery, the innocent partner may seek a divorce and remarry. This is the position of Greek-Orthodox churches. The biblical scholar Raymond E. Brown, however, maintains that a more likely interpretation would find 'un-chastity' to be a reference to marriage within what Jews regarded as the forbidden degrees of kindred.[2] St Paul, in his first

---

1. Genesis 1:27 and 2: 24
2. Raymond E. Brown, *An Introduction to the New Testament*, p 194, Doubleday 1997

letter to the Corinthians,[3] for example, refers to a case of sexual immorality where a man lives with his father's wife. Overall however, it can be said that Jesus simply opposed divorce.

The disciples are appalled. 'If such is the case of a man with his wife, it is better not to marry.' Jesus says to them, 'Not everyone can accept this teaching, but only those to whom it is given.' He raises one possibility, that of abstinence, being 'eunuchs' for the sake of the kingdom of heaven. Both of Jesus' demands may seem to many people impossible to follow. But Jesus says, 'Let anyone accept this who can.' For Jesus' followers, the prohibition of divorce is normative.

People bring little children to Jesus in order that he might lay his hands on them and pray. The disciples speak sternly to those who bring them; but Jesus says, 'Let the little children come to me, and do not stop them; for it is to such as these that the kingdom of heaven belongs.' Jesus is unique among ancient religious and philosophical teachers in recognising children as significant. For Jesus, children represent those who are dependent on God, and are prepared to receive God's love and protection. So it must be for his disciples.

A rich young Jew comes to Jesus, and asks 'What deed must I do to have eternal life? Jesus answers him 'Why do you ask me about what is good? There is only one who is good. If you wish to enter into life keep the commandments.' Jesus seems to envision the possibility of salvation for Jews apart from the route of Christian discipleship. The young man affirms that he has kept the commandments since his youth. Jesus then calls him to discipleship. 'If you wish to be perfect, go, sell your possessions, and give the money to the poor, and you will have treasure in heaven; then come, follow me.' When the wealthy young man hears these words, he goes away sad because, by trusting in his wealth rather than depending on God, like little children, being part of God's kingdom is simply beyond him.

The rich young man, of course, is not a Christian. He is a Jew. Jesus implies that giving up one's possessions is not incumbent

---

3. 1 Corinthians 5:1-2

on all, nor is it presented as absolutely necessary in order to enter eternal life. However, Jesus is warning his own disciples of the dangers of wealth. 'Truly I tell you, it will be hard for a rich person to enter the kingdom of heaven.' Using a Jewish metaphor for overcoming an insuperable difficulty, he says 'It is easier for a camel to go through the eye of a needle than for someone who is rich to enter the kingdom of God.' The disciples are astonished. 'Then who can be saved?' they ask. 'For mortals,' Jesus tells them, 'it is impossible, but for God all things are possible.' In other words, it will take a miracle to get the rich into the kingdom. The miracle will consist in getting them to give up their wealth by sharing it with others.

Peter then asks Jesus, 'Look, we have left everything and followed you. What then will we have?' Jesus says to him, 'Truly I tell you, at the renewal of all things,[4] when the Son of Man is seated on the throne of his glory, you who have followed me will also sit on twelve thrones, judging the twelve tribes of Israel. And everyone who has left houses or brothers or sisters or father, or mother, or children or fields, for my name's sake, will inherit a hundredfold, and will inherit eternal life. But many who are first will be last, and the last will be first.'

Jesus is again emphasising the upside-down character of the kingdom. God's kingdom is not given to the 'first', the most powerful of this world, but to the 'last', who have left behind precious things for the sake of the kingdom.

The parable that follows[5] speaks about vineyard labourers who work in shifts from nine to five, with the latecomers receiving the same pay as those who started work in the morning. The story highlights God's sovereignty, and a graciousness that is not based on what people earn, but on the generosity and goodness of God, and especially on his love for the marginal in Jewish society. That the disciples should have constant care and concern for such people is a constant theme in Matthew's

---

4. The 'new age' or new world, will be ushered in by the full coming of God's kingdom.
5. Matthew 20:1-16

gospel. He repeats the same mantra, 'So the last will be first, and the first will be last.'

As they continue on their journey, Jesus takes the twelve disciples aside, and says to them, 'See, we are going up to Jerusalem, and the Son of Man will be handed over to the chief priests and scribes, and they will condemn him to death; then they will hand him over to the Gentiles to be mocked and flogged and crucified; and on the third day he will be raised.'

Matthew now turns to the question of ambition, always a danger that can beset the church at any time. The mother of Zebedee's sons, James and John, comes with her sons to make a request of Jesus. She wants them to receive positions of power sitting on his right and left in his kingdom. 'You do not know what you are asking,' Jesus answers. 'Are you able to drink the cup (of suffering) that I am about to drink?' They reply, 'We are able.' 'You will indeed drink my cup,[6] but to sit at my right hand and at my left, this is not mine to grant, but it is for those for whom it has been prepared by my Father.'

When the other ten apostles hear of what happened they are angry with the two brothers. But Jesus says to them, 'You know that the rulers of the Gentiles lord it over them, and their great ones are tyrants over them. It will not be so among you; but whoever wishes to be great among you must be your servant, and whoever wishes to be first among you must be your slave; for the Son of Man came not to be served but to serve, and to give his life a ransom for many.' In contrast to those who ambition power and domination, humble service is to be at the heart of Christian leadership if the community, the church, is to be part of God's kingdom.

As Jesus leaves the town of Jericho with a crowd of followers, Matthew tells the story of two blind men who are sitting by a roadside. When they hear that Jesus is passing by, they shout, 'Have mercy on us, Son of David.'[7] The crowd sternly orders

6. Herod Agrippa put James to death about the year 44AD and John too would share in Jesus' suffering.
7. Although there is no record of King David being a healer, there is

them to be quiet, but they shout even more loudly, 'Have mercy on us, Lord, Son of David!' Jesus stops still and calls them over, saying, 'What do you want me to do for you?' They say to him, 'Lord, let our eyes be opened.' Moved with compassion, Jesus touches their eyes. Immediately they regain their sight and they follow him.

Besides the literal meaning of the request by the two blind men that they regain their sight, Jesus is telling his disciples how they too need to have their eyes opened especially as they come to terms with all that is about to happen in Jerusalem. That there can be victory in suffering seems paradoxical. For the disciples to believe that when they see Jesus enduring the agony of crucifixion they see someone who embodies God suffering with humanity, and yet is victorious in spite of it all, will certainly demand that their eyes be opened, and will demand a very deep faith.

---

some evidence that Solomon, a son and successor of David, was regarded as a healer in Judaism at the time the New Testament came to be written.

Jesus Enters Jerusalem
(21)

As Jesus and his disciples approach Bethphage at the Mount of Olives, on the outskirts of Jerusalem, Jesus sends two of his disciples to a nearby village, saying to them, 'You will find a donkey tied, and a colt with her; untie them and bring them to me. If anyone says anything to you, just say this, "The Lord needs them." And he will send them back immediately.'[1] The disciples do as Jesus asks.

Jesus then enters Jerusalem riding on a donkey to be greeted by crowds of people who spread their cloaks on the ground, while others spread branches of trees in his path shouting, 'Blessed is the one who comes in the name of the Lord!'[2] When he enters Jerusalem, the city is in turmoil. 'Who is this?' people ask, and the crowds answer, 'This is the prophet Jesus from Nazareth in Galilee.' Matthew stresses Jesus' meekness and peacefulness, and the jubilation of the crowd as he enters the city. This is in sharp contrast to the crowd that, only a sort time later, will be baying for his blood, shouting 'Crucify him.'

Jesus then enters the Temple in Jerusalem and drives out all those who were selling and buying there; he upsets the tables of the money changers and the chairs of those who are selling pigeons. He says, 'My house shall be called a house of prayer; but you are making it a den of robbers'[3] and he cures the blind and lame people who come to him in the Temple. The chief priests are indignant that people are shouting, 'Hosanna to the Son of David.' 'Do you hear what these are saying?' Jesus says to them,

---

1. Matthew famously mixes up a reference in the prophet Zechariah to a donkey and a colt which are parallel designations for one animal. (9:9)
2. The crowd is quoting Psalm 118:26
3. This is a quote from the prophet Jeremiah (7:11)

'Yes; have you never read, "Out of the mouths of infants and nursing babies you have prepared praise for yourself"?'[4]

Jerusalem was *the* religious centre for the people of Israel because the Temple was there. Pigeons and other animals were sold for sacrifice and debased currency was exchanged for 'harder' currency, the shekel. Jesus' actions show his zeal as a religious reformer, and his disgust with the abuses of a bankrupt system of worship. His words echo the words of the prophet Jeremiah: 'If you truly amend your ways and your doings, if you truly act justly one with another, if you do not oppress the alien, the orphan, and the widow, or shed innocent blood in this place, and if you do not go after other gods to your own hurt, then I will dwell with you in this place, in the land that I gave of old to your ancestors forever and ever … Has this house, which is called by my name, become a den of robbers in your sight?'[5] No wonder that the chief priests were indignant as they realised the full significance of Jesus' implied criticism of their behaviour, and how they permitted the abuses that pertained in the Temple.

The following peculiar story of Jesus cursing a fig tree harks back to words of the prophet Jeremiah. As Jesus returns to the city in the early morning from the village of Bethany, the home of his friends Martha, Mary and Lazarus, he feels hungry. Seeing a fig tree by the road, he goes to it and finds nothing on it but leaves. He says to it, 'May no fruit ever come from you again!' and at that instant the fig tree withers. The disciples are amazed. 'How did the fig tree wither at once?' Jesus answers, 'Truly I tell you, if you have faith and do not doubt, not only will you do what has been done to the fig tree, but even if you say to this mountain, "Be lifted up and thrown into the sea," it will be done. Whatever you ask for in prayer with faith, you will receive.'

In the book of the prophet Jeremiah the Lord says, 'When I wanted to gather them, says the Lord, there are no grapes on the vine, nor figs on the fig tree: even the leaves are withered, and

---

4. Psalm 8:2
5. Jeremiah 7:1-11

what I gave them has passed away from them.'[6] The vine is a symbol for Israel. The fig tree is a symbol for life. The fig, as the sweetest of Levantine fruits, is a biblical symbol of beatitude. So the barren fig tree is a symbol of blighted promise that Jesus uses to represent the failure of the Jewish leadership to renew the life of the people by preferring their own lifeless traditions to the word that God has given them as spoken by Jesus. Such renewed life, he says, will only come about through faith that leads to prayer.

The chief priests and elders ask Jesus, 'By what authority are you doing these things, and who gave you this authority?' They hope to force Jesus into an admission that his power comes directly from God, thus opening himself up to the charge of blasphemy. He answers by asking them why they had refused to believe John the Baptist. Because the people revered John, and because they were afraid of the crowd, the priests and elders simply reply, 'We do not know.' Jesus says, 'Neither will I tell you by what authority I am doing these things.'

He tells them a parable about two sons who are asked by their father to go and work in his vineyard. The first refuses, but later changes his mind. The second says he will go, but does not. 'Which of the two did the will of his father?' Jesus asks. 'The first', they answer. 'Truly I tell you, the tax collectors and prostitutes are going into the kingdom of God ahead of you. For John came to you in the way of righteousness and you did not believe him, but the tax collectors and prostitutes believed him; and even after you saw it, you did not change your minds and believe him.' No wonder the chief priests and elders hate him so much.

Driving home his message to the chief priests and elders, Jesus tells them another parable about wicked tenants. 'There was a landowner who planted a vineyard, put a fence around it, dug a wine press in it, and built a watchtower.[7] Then he leased it

---

6. Jeremiah 8:13
7. 'Let me sing for my beloved my love-song concerning his vineyard: My beloved had a vineyard on a very fertile hill. He dug it and cleared it of stones, and planted it with choice vines; he built a watchtower in

to tenants and went to another country. When the harvest time had come, he sent his slaves to the tenants to collect his produce. But the tenants seized his slaves and beat one, killed another and stoned another. Next he sent more slaves, more than the first; and they treated them in the same way. Finally he sent his son to them, saying 'They will respect my son.' But when the tenants saw the son, they said to themselves, 'This is the heir; come, let us kill him and get his inheritance.' So they seized him, threw him out of the vineyard, and killed him. Now when the owner of the vineyard comes, what will he do to those tenants?' The chief priests and elders answer, 'He will put those wretches to a miserable death, and lease the vineyard to other tenants, who will give him the produce at harvest time.' Are the chief priests and elders unwittingly describing the fate that will descend on them when the Romans conquer Jerusalem?

The chief priests and elders surely get the message. The landowner is God. The vineyard is Israel. The tenants are the chief priests and elders. The slaves are the prophets who have so often been rejected by Israel's leaders. The son is clearly Jesus for whose death the chief priests and elders will be held responsible. Harvest time is the kingdom come in all its fullness.

Jesus goes on, 'Have you never read in the scriptures: "The stone that the builders rejected has become the cornerstone; this was the Lord's doing, and it is amazing in our eyes."[8] Therefore I tell you, the kingdom of God will be taken away from you and given to a people that produce the fruits of the kingdom.'

The leaders of tribes and peoples are sometimes called 'cornerstones' in the Jewish scriptures.[9] But Jesus is now the cornerstone, the foundation on which his community of disciples, his church, is to be built. The chief priests and leaders reject God's latest prophet, Jesus himself, and so close themselves off from participation in God's kingdom, God's Rule. Instead the king-

---

the midst of it, and hewed out a wine vat in it; he expected it to yield grapes, but it yielded wild grapes.' Isaiah 5: 2
8. Psalm 118:22-23
9. Isaiah 19:13: Zechariah 10:4

dom is welcomed by 'a people who produce its fruits'. Matthew may well have had in mind the believing Jews and the converted Gentiles who were members of his own community, who, as he sees it, form the new people of God, the true Israel.

Entrapment
(22)

Jesus is addressing the chief priests and the Pharisees. He tells them a parable about a son's wedding feast to which a king has invited some guests. The invited guests are not interested and refuse to attend: one goes off to his farm, another to his business, and the rest seize the king's servants, maltreat and kill them. The king is furious. He dispatches his troops, destroys the murderers and burns their town. He then sends his servants to the cross-roads to invite everyone they can find to attend the wedding. The servants do as they are asked, and collect everyone they can find, bad and good alike.

However, when the king comes in to look at the guests, one man is not wearing a wedding garment. The king says, 'Friend, how did you get in here without a wedding robe?' But the man is silent. So the king says to the attendants, 'Bind him hand and foot, and throw him out into the outer darkness, where there will be weeping and grinding of teeth.' And, Jesus adds, 'Many are called but few are chosen.'

The king in this parable is God. The son is Jesus. The wedding feast is God's kingdom banquet, to which God invites whomever he pleases. The servants are the prophets who have been maltreated and murdered. The invited guests are the chief priests and Pharisees. The Jewish leaders refuse to accept Jesus, and they despise the outcasts of Israel, the tax collectors and those in despised trades, whom Jesus calls 'the little ones' whom he invites to the feast of God's kingdom.

In God's kingdom there will be no prestige, no status, no division of people into inferior and superior; all are to be loved and respected: one's education, wealth, ancestry, authority or rank will be of no importance. The chief priests and Pharisees, who cannot live without feeling superior to at least some people, will simply not be at home in God's kingdom where beggars, former prostitutes, servants, women and children are treated as their equals.

In Jesus' story of the wedding banquet, the man without a wedding garment symbolises those members of the Christian community who do something grave and notorious, and refuse to listen to the community and repent their ways. They are to be treated as outsiders, expelled from the community, and 'thrown into the outer darkness' like rowdy guests at a party.

What does Jesus mean by saying that 'many are called, but few are chosen'? Both good and bad Jews and Gentiles enter the Christian community; but the 'many' who have accepted the initial call have to face further judgement. Unworthy Christians will suffer the same fate as those who initially accepted God's reign but were not worthy of it.[1] For Matthew it is never a question of the church replacing Israel; rather it is the replacement of the 'many' unworthy Jews, especially their leaders, by a community of Jews and Gentiles who believe in Jesus, those who are 'chosen', and have responded positively to his demands for participation in God's kingdom

The Pharisees send some of their disciples and some Herodians, supporters of the Herodian dynasty, and therefore the most suitable people to report to the Roman authorities, in the hope of inducing Jesus to say something against Caesar. 'Tell us what you think, is it lawful to pay taxes to the emperor or not?' Jesus replies, 'Why are you putting me to the test, you hypocrites? Show me the coin used for the tax.' Jesus asks for a Roman coin, a denarius with Caesar's head on it, and says, 'Give therefore to the emperor the things that are the emperor's, and to God the things that are God's.'

The tax, the equivalent of a full day's pay for a labourer, was a sort of 'poll tax', a prerequisite for living peacefully as a subject

---

1. 'I tell you, many will come from east and west and will eat with Abraham and Isaac and Jacob in the kingdom of heaven, while the heirs of the kingdom will be thrown into the outer darkness.' Matthew 8:11-12

of the Roman emperor. It was a source of political discontent among Jews. While the Pharisees and Herodians accepted the imposition of the tax, ardent nationalists opposed it. If Jesus were to oppose the tax, he would get into trouble with the Romans. If he agrees to pay it, he would lose face with the nationalists. Jesus avoids this pitfall by recommending paying the tax on the grounds that it is the emperor's coinage to begin with – so long as this does not encroach on what is owed to the overriding authority of God. He skilfully avoids the question of co-operation with or resistance to the Roman government.

That same day some Sadducees, who deny there is a resurrection, approach him and put this question to him, 'Teacher, Moses said, "If a man dies childless, his brother shall marry his widow, and raise up children for his brother. Now there were seven brothers among us; the first married, and died childless leaving the widow to his brother. The second did the same, so also the third, down to the seventh. Last of all, the woman herself died. In the resurrection, then, whose wife of the seven will she be? For all of them married her".'

Jesus answers them, 'You are wrong, because you know neither the scriptures nor the power of God. For in the resurrection they neither marry nor are given in marriage, but are like the angels in heaven. And as for the resurrection of the dead, have you not read what was said to you by God: 'I am the God of Abraham, the God of Isaac and the God of Jacob?'[2] He is God, not of the dead, but of the living.' And when the crowd hear it, they are astounded at his teaching. While the Jewish leaders continue to be hostile to Jesus, the Jewish crowds are amazed at Jesus' ability to outwit his opponents.

The Pharisees now try another tack. To disconcert Jesus, one of them, probably a lawyer, asks, 'Teacher, which commandment in the Law is the greatest?' Jesus responds, 'You shall love the Lord your God with all your heart, and with all your soul, and with all your mind.[3] This is the greatest and first command-

---

2. Exodus 3:6
3. Jesus is quoting from Deuteronomy 6:5.

ment. And the second is like it: 'You shall love your neighbour as yourself.'[4] On these two commandments hang all the law and the prophets.'

The Torah had some 613 precepts. This presented a problem for those who took them to be the revelation of God's will for Israel. Are some precepts more important than others? Jesus proclaims that *love* of God and neighbour is the most important teaching of the Torah. By 'love' he means fidelity to the Covenant, the bond of union between God and the chosen people. It's a question of willing and doing what is required to further that bond with all one's heart, will, soul, and mind. The rabbis taught that union with God hung on the Torah, Temple service, and deeds of loving-kindness. The originality of Jesus lies in the combination of these two commandments, and asserting that on them the law and the teaching of the prophets depend.

Finally Jesus turns the tables on the Pharisees. 'What do you think of the Messiah? Whose son is he?' They say to him, 'The son of David.' Jesus says, 'How is it then that David by the Spirit,[5] calls him Lord, saying "The Lord said to my Lord, sit at my right hand, until I put your enemies under your feet"?'[6] If David thus calls him Lord, how can he be his son?'

Jesus' somewhat puzzling answer is based on Psalm 110:1. That King David spoke prophetically through the Psalms is essential to his argument. In the Psalms David talks about Yahweh, the Lord God, speaking to 'my lord', a new king. If David calls the new king 'lord,' here understood to be the future Messiah, then the figure about whom he speaks must be more than David's son.[7] What Jesus is saying is that the usual conviction that the Messiah would be David's son does not go far enough. If the Pharisees had traced the Messiah's human origin back to David, they should see that there was something divine about

---

4. Leviticus 19:18

5. 'David by the Spirit' reflects the Jewish belief that King David spoke under God's inspiration.

6. Psalm 110:1

7. Jeremiah 23:5

the Messiah to set him above David. An identity between Jesus' lordship and Yahweh's lordship is being suggested since Jesus is the Messiah and he is also Son of David, Lord, and Son of God.

The Pharisees find themselves unable to counter Jesus' many arguments and, Matthew tells us, from that day none dared to ask him any more questions.

Denunciations
(23)

Matthew introduces a lengthy polemic against those Jewish leaders who refuse to accept Jesus' teaching.[1] The context in which Matthew is writing is probably the conflict between Jewish Christians and their more powerful opponents, represented by the scribes and Pharisees, who were strong rivals to Matthew's community.

Jesus says to the crowds and his disciples, 'The scribes and Pharisees sit on Moses' seat; therefore, do whatever they teach you, and follow it; but do not do as they do, for they do not practise what they teach. They tie up heavy burdens, hard to bear, and lay them on the shoulders of others; but they themselves are unwilling to lift a finger to move them.'

'Moses' seat' is probably a metaphor for the teaching and ruling authority of the scribes and Pharisees. The rather startling command to 'Do as they say, but not do as they do' is extraordinary given that Jesus had previously criticised their sayings and their traditions.[2] While much of the Jewish leaders' teaching is sound, at least in showing zeal for God and the Jewish scriptures, the assumption is that their practice leaves much to be desired. The 'burdens' they lay on people are probably the applica-

---

1. Such hostile criticism is not untypical of one Jewish group by another Jewish group in the first century AD. However, one has to be careful not to tarnish all Pharisees or scribes with the one brush, many of whom were sensitive and ethical people. In the gospels they get a bad press. They represent all those who are opposed to Jesus, and become symbols of attitudes that Matthew did not want Christian leaders to imitate.
2. Matthew 16:11-12

tion of priestly purity laws to everyday life, and their stress on tithing and Sabbath observance.[3]

Jesus continues, 'They love to have the place of honour at banquets and the best seats in the synagogues, and to be greeted with respect in the market places, and to have people call them rabbi. But you are not to be called rabbi, for you have one teacher, and you are all students. And call no one your father, for you have one Father – the one in heaven. Nor are you to be called instructors, for you have one instructor, the Messiah. The greatest among you will be your servant. And all who exalt themselves will be humbled, and all who humble themselves will be exalted. '

Why are Jesus' disciples not to be called rabbi or father? The word Rabbi means 'My Lord,' a title of honour in use in the first century: it could also mean teacher. For Matthew, Jesus is the supreme Lord and teacher. The Aramaic title 'Father' was used for elders, and the dead who were revered. Matthew associates the title with God alone.[4]

Jesus turns on the scribes and Pharisees, listing a number of woes, prophetic denunciations, as the ancient prophets did. 'Woe to you, scribes and Pharisees, hypocrites! For you lock people out of the kingdom of heaven. For you do not go in yourselves, and when others are going in, you stop them.' Jesus accuses the Jewish leaders of preventing the spread of the gospel, 'locking' people out of the kingdom as preached by Jesus, urging them not to follow him.

---

3. Such purity laws may refer to ritual immersion for conversion or following menstruation, hand washing and the keeping of implements or food kosher. While rejecting the system as a whole, Christianity did retain ritual immersion in baptism.

4. Raymond E. Brown makes the point that anti-Catholic literalists have appealed to this passage in criticising the practice of addressing priests as 'Father', even though they seem to have no problem of addressing learned people as 'Professor' or 'Doctor,' which are the modern equivalents of 'Rabbi' and 'Teacher'. Matthew's text criticises a love of being honoured – a love that finds expression in different titles in different times. The real lesson is that, no matter what title is used, 'all are brothers and sisters' in Christ, and the greatest must be a servant. (*An Introduction to the New Testament*, Doubleday, 1996)

'You cross sea and land to make a single convert, and you make the new convert twice as much a child of hell as yourselves.' This quotation may be a reference by Matthew to Jewish missionary activity after the destruction of the Temple by the Romans in AD70.

'Woe to you blind guides, who say, "Whoever swears by the sanctuary (the Temple) is bound by nothing, but whoever swears by the gold of the sanctuary is bound by the oath." You blind fools! For which is greater, the gold or the sanctuary that has made the gold sacred?' The Jews, out of reverence, did not like to mention the name of God, so their leaders found ways around that by swearing by the Temple, the gold in the Temple, or its altar. Jesus cuts through these quibbles to argue that any real oath demands the intention of appealing to God.

Jesus turns to the custom of tithing, which meant setting aside one-tenth of the produce of the land to be given to the poor. 'Woe to you scribes and Pharisees, hypocrites! For you tithe mint, dill and cumin, and have neglected the weightier matters of the law: justice and mercy and faith. It is these you ought to have practised without neglecting the others.' While Jesus criticises the extension of tithing to include even spices, at the same time he asks for compliance with what the Jewish scriptures demand.[5]

'You blind guides! You strain out a gnat but swallow a camel!' Camels were regarded as unclean animals and therefore could not be eaten by Jews. The irony is heightened by Jesus' insistence that those who claim to be the most observant Jews, the leaders, miss the most important matters, justice, mercy and faith.

'Woe to you, scribes and Pharisees, hypocrites! For you clean the outside of the cup and of the plate, but inside they are full of greed and self-indulgence.' Jesus is appealing for interior purity of heart and mind. He accuses the leaders of being like whitewashed tombs full of bones, hypocrisy and lawlessness.

'Woe to you, scribes and Pharisees, hypocrites! For you build

5. Deuteronomy 14:23

the tombs of the prophets and decorate the graves of the righteous,[6] and you say, "If we had lived in the days of our ancestors, we would not have taken part with them in shedding the blood of the prophets." Thus you testify against yourselves that you are descendants of those who murdered the prophets.' In others words, the scribes and Pharisees who challenge Jesus will continue to do what their ancestors did in the past, shed the blood of the innocent, like that of the prophet Jesus himself.

'Fill up, then, the measure of your ancestors.' This refers to the quota of evil that must be filled before the final judgement. 'You snakes, you brood of vipers!'[7] 'How can you escape being sentenced to hell? Therefore I send you prophets, sages, and scribes, some of whom you will kill and crucify, and some you will flog in your synagogues and pursue from town to town, so that upon you may come all the righteous blood shed on earth, from the blood of the righteous Abel to the blood of Zechariah son of Barachiah, whom you murdered between the sanctuary and the altar. Truly I tell you, all this will come upon this generation.'

Jesus, or perhaps Matthew with hindsight, is warning the scribes and Pharisees of the impending hellish destruction of Jerusalem in AD70 by the Romans, which would be understood as a punishment for persecuting the ancient prophets from Abel, in the book of Genesis, to the blood of Zechariah killed between the sanctuary and the altar.'[8] 'All this', the destruction of Jerusalem, will come in the lifetime of Jesus' audience. But Matthew also has in mind the sufferings that members of his church are undergoing as well as Jesus' crucifixion.

Jesus laments the impending doom of Jerusalem. 'Jerusalem, Jerusalem, the city that kills the prophets and stones those who are sent to it! How often have I desired to gather your children together as a hen gathers her brood under her wings, and you

---

6. It is said that in Jesus' time there was a large-scale project to build monuments to the heroes of ancient Israel.
7. Jesus uses the same term as John the Baptist in Matthew 3:7
8. 11 Chronicles 24:20-22

were not willing! See, your house is left to you, desolate. For I tell you, you will not see me again until you say, "Blessed is the one who comes in the name of the Lord".'

Jesus had hoped to gather the citizens of the city into God's kingdom, but large numbers are unwilling to accept his invitation. The 'house that is left desolate' refers to Jerusalem and its Temple which will be destroyed by the Romans. Finally, Jesus says that the citizens of Jerusalem will not see him again until he returns at the end of time, when they will greet him, once again, in the words of Psalm 118, 'Blessed is the one who comes in the name of the Lord.'[9] Jesus' return will be a major theme in the next two chapters of Matthew's gospel.

---

9. Psalm 118:26

The End Is Nigh
(24-25)

One day, as Jesus is leaving the Temple area in Jerusalem, his disciples draw his attention to the Temple buildings. Jesus says to them, 'You see all these, do you not? Truly I tell you, not one stone will be left here upon another: all will be thrown down.' Jesus is talking about the future destruction of Herod's Temple which was burned down in AD70. Such a catastrophe seems to the disciples to portend the end of the world as they know it, and so they ask Jesus, 'Tell us, when will this be, and what will be the sign of your coming and of the end of the age?'

Matthew's text weaves together two separate events into the fabric of his story: the destruction of the Temple in Jerusalem by the Romans and the final coming of Christ at the end of time. After various uprisings by the Jews, Jerusalem was besieged by the Romans under Vespasian and Titus in AD70 and suffered substantial destruction. The siege proper began in the spring. By September the city was finally taken, plundered, and razed. Titus had wanted to spare the Temple, demanding Jewish surrender as his price, but they refused and further fighting ensued. A soldier cast a blazing brand into one of the Temple chambers, and the Temple was destroyed. The destruction of Jerusalem meant much more than the mere levelling of the holy city. It brought to an end the ancient tradition according to which sacrifice was offered to Yahweh only in Jerusalem, making it the centre of the Jewish world.

This is the background to Matthew's account that was written somewhere between 80 and 90AD, probably in the Antioch region, some ten to twenty years after the destruction of the Jerusalem Temple. This was such an enormous shock to Matthew's Christians that they were sure that the end of the world was in sight. As we will see, many of Jesus' admonitions about the end times clearly have meaning for Matthew's community. Talk of new messiahs, of people falling away, of disciples being hated, of mutual betrayal, and of love growing cold, are all dangers that beset Matthew's community.

Jesus warns the disciples, 'Beware that no one leads you astray. For many will come in my name, saying "I am the Messiah!" and they will lead many astray. And you will hear of wars and rumours of wars; see that you are not alarmed; for this must take place, but the end is not yet. For nation will rise against nation, and kingdom against kingdom, and there will be famines and earthquakes in various places: all this is but the beginning of the birth pangs.'

Jewish literature used the metaphor of 'birth pangs' to describe the coming of the messianic kingdom. The sufferings that people will endure until the 'end time' are compared to the onset of labour pains that a woman endures in giving birth.

'Then they will hand you over to be tortured and will put you to death, and you will be hated by all nations because of my name. Then many will fall away, and they will betray one another and hate one another. And many false prophets will arise and lead many astray. And because of the increase of lawlessness, the love of many will grow cold. But the one who endures to the end will be saved. And this good news of the kingdom will be proclaimed throughout the world, as a testimony to all the nations; and then the end will come.' The whole world means the Graeco-Roman world, and by 70AD the gospel had already reached the main parts of the Roman Empire. The persecution envisioned by Matthew probably refers to both Jewish leaders and Gentiles as persecutors.

'So when you see the desolating sacrilege standing in the holy place, as was spoken of by the prophet Daniel[1] (let the reader understand), then those in Judea must flee to the mountains; the one on the housetop must not go down to take what is in the house; the one in the field must not turn back to get a coat. Woe

---

1. Daniel 9:27

to those who are pregnant and to those who are nursing infants in those days! Pray that your flight may not be in winter or on a Sabbath.[2] For at that time there will be great suffering, such as has not been from the beginning of the world until now, no, and never will be.'

The 'desolating sacrilege' probably refers to a threat by the emperor Caligula in AD40 to set up a statue of himself in the Jerusalem Temple. The reader is to 'understand' that Matthew, for good political reason, does not wish to mention the Romans by name, the very ones who bring desolation to Jerusalem. But when that time comes, people must get away quickly from the city and flee to the hills. Matthew is using the historical fact of the destruction of Jerusalem to highlight what the 'end time' will be like when the Messiah returns.

'And if those days had not been short, no one would be saved; but for the sake of the elect those days will be cut short.' God will cut short the days of suffering on account of the 'elect', those whom God loves. God is in control, so there is no reason to despair even in the midst of tribulations.

Jesus then repeats that the disciples should beware of false messiahs and false prophets, who may even deceive God's chosen ones. 'Take note, I have told you beforehand. So if they say to you, "Look! He is in the wilderness," do not go out. If they say, "Look! He is in the inner rooms," do not believe it. For as the lightning comes from the east and flashes as far as the west, so will be the coming of the Son of Man. Wherever the corpse is, there the vultures will gather.' The coming of the Son of Man will not be hidden. His coming will be as clear and public as lightning flashing across the sky, or as vultures gathering around carrion.

'Immediately after the suffering of those days the sun will be darkened, and the moon will not give its light: the stars will fall

---

2. In winter travel in Palestine was difficult because of the rains. The reference to the Sabbath indicates that it was still observed by Matthew's community. Jews were not allowed to take long journeys on the Sabbath; to do so could well provoke a crisis of conscience.

from heaven, and the powers of heaven will be shaken.[3] In other words, cosmic signs will herald the coming of the Son of Man.

'Then the sign of the Son of Man will appear in heaven, and then all the tribes of the earth will mourn, and they will see the Son of Man coming on the clouds of heaven with power and great glory. And he will send out his angels with a loud trumpet call, and they will gather his elect from the four winds, from one end of heaven to the other.'

Jesus is using Old Testament references from the prophets Isaiah, Daniel and Zechariah. 'The Lord will raise a signal for the nations, and will assemble the outcasts of Israel, and gather the dispersed of Judah from the four corners of the earth.'[4] Daniel writes, 'I saw one like a human being coming on the clouds of heaven.'[5] Matthew, of course, is referring to the Son of Man, Jesus, who will come on the clouds of heaven, a symbol for the presence of God. That the tribes will mourn may be a reference to the prophet Zechariah: 'I will pour out a spirit of compassion and supplication on the house of David and the inhabitants of Jerusalem, so that, when they look on the one they have pierced, they shall mourn for him, as one mourns for an only child, and weep bitterly over him, as one weeps over a firstborn.'[6] Matthew's readers will surely spot a reference to Jesus' death.

Jesus continues, 'From the fig tree learn its lesson: as soon as its branch becomes tender and puts forth its leaves, you know the summer is near. So also, when you see all these things, you know that he is near, at the very gates. Truly I tell you, this generation will not pass until all these things will have taken place. Heaven and earth will pass away, but my words will not pass away.'[7] Jesus' solemn saying echoes the words of the prophet Isaiah, 'The grass withers, the flower fades; but the word of God will stand forever.' Jesus' statement that 'this generation will not

---

3. Isaiah 13:10
4. Isaiah 11:12
5. Daniel 7:13
6. Zechariah 12:10
7. Isaiah 40:8

pass away until all these things will have taken place' is puzzling. Perhaps he is referring to the destruction of Jerusalem, or to his own death and resurrection. It can hardly apply to the end of the world.

Only now does Jesus answer the disciples' question about the end of the world. 'But about that day and hour, no one knows it, neither the angels in heaven, nor the Son, but only the Father.' Jesus received from his Father the knowledge that had to do with his mission. However, as he explicitly states, because he is a human being, he does not know all the elements of God's plans for humanity.

Jesus gives various warnings as to how the disciples are to behave until the Messiah's final return. They are to be on the alert because he will come 'at an unexpected hour'. He tells a parable of an unfaithful servant who spends his time eating and drinking with drunkards while his master is away. 'The master will cut him off and put him with the hypocrites, where there will be weeping and gnashing of teeth.'[8] In other words, unfaithful Christians, and more specifically their leaders, will be judged no less harshly than the scribes and Pharisees, and may be excommunicated from the community. The 'weeping and gnashing of teeth' refers to the anguish and sadness of being left out of God's kingdom.

Jesus' parable of the ten bridesmaids,[9] especially those who are not prepared for the master's delayed return to his home after his wedding, is a warning to the disciples: 'You must be ready, for the Son of Man is coming at an unexpected hour.' The point is that, even if the Son of Man is slow in returning, nonetheless his disciples must be watchful and ready for him whenever he comes, 'with their lamps lit', that is, full of good works.

The parable of the talents[10] speaks of the importance of using God's gifts, especially the Torah, wisely and fruitfully. When

---

8. Matthew 24: 45-51
9. Matthew 25:1ff
10. A huge, unspecified amount of money.

Jesus says that, 'for all those who have, more will be given, and they will have an abundance; but from those who have nothing, even what they have will be taken away,' we may well be puzzled. Jesus' message is not one about meriting reward, or using talents to the best of one's ability, but about dedicated and fruitful response to God's gifts in and through Jesus. To those followers who fruitfully receive God's word, and put it into action, an abundance of insight and blessings will be given. Jesus' opponents, on the other hand, who refuse to accept his teaching, will lose even what they have, a full understanding of how Jesus' words and deeds are the fulfilment of the Jewish scriptures.

There follows the famous passage, found only in Matthew, of the Judgement of the Nations. In apocalyptic terms it pictures the Son of Man judging the nations of the world. 'When the Son of Man comes in his glory and all the angels with him, then he will sit on his throne of glory. All the nations will be gathered before him, and he will separate people one from another as a shepherd separates the sheep from the goats, and he will put the sheep on his right hand and the goats at the left.'

It is an interesting fact that no mention is made here of the twelve apostles whom Jesus had previously said would judge the twelve tribes of Israel, that is, the whole nation. 'Truly I tell you, at the renewal of all things, when the Son of Man is seated on the throne of his glory, you who have followed me will also sit on twelve thrones, judging the twelve tribes of Israel.'[11] It seems that the word 'nations' here must refer to the Gentiles. So there will be separate judgements for Israel and for Gentiles: the Gentiles will be judged by their deeds of mercy towards the disciples of Jesus, because such deeds will be taken as done to Jesus himself. As Jesus had said to his disciple, 'Whoever welcomes you welcomes me, and whoever welcomes me welcomes the one who sent me.'[12]

St Paul too speaks of separate judgements for Jews and Gentiles. God, on the day of wrath, 'will repay according to each

______

11. Matthew 19:28
12. Matthew 10:40

one's deeds: to those who by patiently doing good seek for glory and honour and immortality, he will give eternal life; while those who are self-seeking and who obey not the truth but wickedness, there will be wrath and fury. There will be anguish and distress for everyone who does evil, the Jew first and also the Greek, but glory and honour and peace for everyone who does good, the Jew first and also the Greek. For God shows no partiality.'[13]

The Gentiles will be judged by their deeds of mercy done to the followers of Christ. He will say to those nations who do evil, 'I was hungry and you gave me no food, I was thirsty and you gave me nothing to drink, I was a stranger and you did not welcome me, naked and you did not give me clothing, sick and in prison and you did not visit me.' Finally he adds, 'Truly I tell you, just as you did not do it to one of the least of these, you did not do it to me.' And, Matthew adds, these will go into eternal punishment, but the righteous into eternal life. No doubt Jesus' admonitions apply equally to his own followers also.

Jesus lived at a time when it seemed that the world was about to come to an end; that it was on the brink of an apocalyptic catastrophe. This was what gave such urgency to his mission. Today we are faced with new threats: diminishing natural resources, and pollution of our environment, war and escalating violence. The problem is that we have built up an all-inclusive political and economic system based on certain assumptions and values that we now realise are bringing us to the point of disaster. Jesus' concern about an impending disaster makes his insights into what must be done all the more relevant today. We may not presume that he had all the answers, but we will ignore his insights and his system of values at our peril.

---

13. Romans 2:5-11

CHAPTER TWENTY

Darkness over the Land
(26-27)

The chief priests and the elders assemble in the palace of the high priest, Caiaphas, and conspire to arrest Jesus by stealth, and have him put to death. However, they are acutely conscious of Jesus' popularity, and so they agree that this should not happen during the Passover festivities as it might cause a riot among the people. However, Judas' treachery may have forced their hands.

Passover time was the annual spring celebration of Israel's liberation from slavery in Egypt. Many pilgrims from all over Israel and from abroad would come to the Jerusalem Temple which, in Jesus' time, was the centre of the Passover celebration. Given that the theme of liberation was central to the festivities, the possibility of an uprising was always present. This is why the Roman Governor, Pontius Pilate, came into town to supervise the crowds and immediately put down any potential uprising.

Jesus is in Bethany, a village about two miles from the city. He is staying in the house of one Simon the leper, possibly someone who had been cured by Jesus. An unknown woman with an alabaster jar of very costly ointment comes in, and pours it on his head as he sits at table. When Jesus' disciples see this, they are angry. 'Why this waste? For this ointment could have been sold for a large sum, and the money given to the poor.' Jesus is aware of their mutterings. 'Why do you trouble the woman? She has performed a very good service for me. For you always have the poor with you, but you will not always have me. By pouring this ointment on my head she has prepared me for burial. Truly I tell you, wherever this good news is proclaimed in the whole world, what she has done will be told in remembrance of her.'

This 'wastage' of good money, and his own greed, prompt

Judas, one of the Twelve, to go to the chief priests and say, 'What will you give me if I betray him to you?' They pay him thirty pieces of silver (the value placed on a slave gored by an ox!) and from that moment Judas looks for an opportune time to betray Jesus.

On the first day of Unleavened Bread,[1] the disciples ask Jesus where he wants to celebrate the Passover. He tells them to go into the city where they will meet a certain man, and they are to say to him, 'My time is near; I will keep the Passover at your house with my disciples.' Given the large crowds in the city, getting a place in which to eat the Passover meal could have been a problem, but it seems that Jesus had already foreseen the problem, and had made his own arrangements. The disciples do as Jesus directs, and they prepare the Passover meal.

When it is evening Jesus reclines with the twelve[2] and while they are eating, he announces, 'One of you will betray me.' One can imagine the disciples' shock. Each one in turn says, 'Surely not I, Lord?' Jesus answers, 'The one who has dipped his hand into the bowl with me will betray me.[3] The Son of Man goes as it is written of him, but woe to that one by whom the Son of Man is betrayed! It would be better for that one not to have been born!' Judas, who has already betrayed him, says, 'Surely not I, Rabbi?' Jesus simply replies, 'You have said so.'

Judas calls Jesus 'Rabbi', a term that Jesus has previously forbidden his disciples to use.[4] Unlike the other disciples, Judas refuses to call Jesus Lord. When Jesus says, 'You have said so,' he is simply confirming the truth of what Judas has said. Judas expects a negative answer. Instead he gets a positive one. Jesus will later use the same expression, 'you have said so,' when answering the high priest's questions.

1. This is another name for Passover. It was the Jewish practice to eat bread without leaven during the eight days of the Passover festival.
2. Individual couches were used for festive banquets and for the reception of honoured guests. The Jews took over this custom from the Greeks.
3 'Even my bosom friend in whom I trusted, who ate my bread, has lifted the heel against me.' Psalm 41:9
4. Matthew 23:8

While they are eating the Passover meal, Jesus takes a loaf of bread, blesses and breaks it, and gives it to the disciples, saying, 'Take, eat; this is my body.' Then he takes a cup, and after giving thanks, he gives it to them saying, 'Drink from it, all of you; for this is my blood of the covenant, which is poured out for many for the forgiveness of sins. I tell you, I will never again drink of this fruit of the vine until that day when I drink it new with you in my Father's kingdom.'

Jesus gives new meaning to what was customary at Passover meals – a blessing, thanksgiving to God, and the sharing of a loaf of bread and a cup of wine. Sharing in Jesus' bread is an invitation to share in his death. Drinking from the cup is an invitation to share in his fate. When he refers to the 'blood of the covenant,' which his disciples are to drink, he is indirectly referring to the book of Exodus where Moses seals God's covenant with Israel by sprinkling the people with an animal's blood,[5] and to the prophet Isaiah who describes the suffering of God's servant.[6]

Passover was a celebration of liberation from Egypt. The meal that Jesus shares with his disciples will produce a new kind of liberation: his death and resurrection will liberate his followers from the fear of death and, by liberating them from their sins, he will unite them in a new covenant of love with the Father.

When Jesus says that he will not drink wine again 'until that day when I drink it new with you in my Father's kingdom,' he is anticipating the final banquet that he and the disciples will share in God's kingdom.

Having sung a hymn at the end of the supper,[7] Jesus and his disciples go to the Mount of Olives, a hill to the east of

---

5. 'See the blood of the covenant that the Lord has made with you.' Exodus 24:8
6. 'He poured out himself to death, and was numbered with the transgressors; yet he bore the sin of many, and made intercession for the transgressors.' Isaiah 53:12
7. The Passover meal traditionally ended with the singing of Psalms 113-118, the so-called great Hallel.

Jerusalem. Jesus tells them, 'You will all become deserters because of me this night; for it is written, "I will strike the shepherd, and the sheep of the flock will be scattered".'[8] Jesus' death will be a severe testing of their faith because they still believe that Jesus is the earthly Messiah whose approaching triumph they are expecting.

Peter asserts that even though the others may lose faith, he never will. But Jesus answers him, 'Truly, I tell you, this very night, before the cock crows, you will deny me three times.' Peter answers, 'Even though I must die with you, I will never deny you.' And all the disciples say the same. The irony is, of course, that Peter will deny Jesus, and the other disciples will flee.

Jesus now moves on to Gethsemane, a small estate at the foot of the Mount of Olives. 'Sit here', he says, 'while I go over there and pray.' He takes Peter, James and John with him. He says to them, 'I am deeply grieved, even to death; remain here, and stay awake with me.' Going off a little further by himself, he throws himself on the ground and prays. 'My Father, if it is possible, let this cup (of suffering) pass from me; yet not what I want but what you want.'

He goes back to the three disciples but finds them asleep. He says to Peter, 'So, could you not stay awake with me one hour? Stay awake and pray that you may not come to the hour of trial,[9] the spirit is willing, but the flesh is weak.' He goes apart again, and prays, 'My Father, if this cannot pass unless I drink it, your will be done.' Jesus, like any man, instinctively fears suffering and death and seeks to escape it but he stifles the instinct and surrenders himself to his Father's will that he fulfil his mission. He returns to the disciples again and finds them asleep. He moves off again and prays for the third time, using the same prayers. Then he comes to the disciples, and says to them, 'Are you still sleeping and taking your rest? See, the hour is at hand,

---

8. Zechariah 13:7
9. The hour of trial is the great testing that accompanies the final coming of God's kingdom.

and the Son of Man is betrayed into the hands of sinners. Get up, let us be going. See, my betrayer is at hand.'

Judas arrives with a large number of men armed with swords and clubs, sent by the chief priests and elders. Judas gives them a sign, saying, 'The one I will kiss is the man; arrest him.' He comes up to Jesus and says, 'Greetings, Rabbi!' and kisses him. Interestingly, Jesus still greets him as a friend. 'Friend, do what you are here to do.'

As Jesus is being arrested, one of Jesus' followers draws his sword and cuts off the ear of one of the high priest's servants. Jesus immediately rebukes him. 'Put your sword back into its place; for all who take the sword will perish by the sword. Do you think that I cannot appeal to my Father, and he will at once send me more than twelve legions of angels?'[10] He had taught openly in the Temple, he says, and is now being arrested as if he were a bandit. 'Day after day I sat in the temple teaching, and you did not arrest me. But all this has taken place so that the scriptures of the prophets may be fulfilled.' Then, Matthew tells us, all the disciples deserted him, and fled.

Jesus is led away to face Caiaphas the high priest and the scribes and elders. Peter follows him at a distance, and sits with the guards in the courtyard of the high priest's house to see how it all will end. Several false witnesses come forward only to be discredited. Eventually two step forward and assert, 'This man said, "I am able to destroy the temple of God and to build it up in three days".' Caiaphas challenges Jesus to answer this charge but he remains silent.

Caiaphas then puts Jesus under oath to compel him to say whether he is the Messiah, the Son of God. Jesus says to him, 'You have said so. But I tell you, from now on you will see the Son of Man seated at the right hand of Power (God) and coming on the clouds of heaven',[11] that is, coming from God, thereby claiming divine status. As far as Caiaphas and the scribes and elders are concerned Jesus has blasphemed, and so deserves to

10. Some 72,000
11. Daniel 7:13

die. Then the members of the Sanhedrin spit in Jesus' face and strike him; and some slap him, saying 'Prophesy to us, you Messiah! Who is it that struck you?'

Meanwhile Peter, having quietly followed Jesus, is sitting outside in the courtyard of the high priest's palace. Two servant girls and a bystander accuse him of being a follower of Jesus. Three times, cursing and swearing, Peter denies the accusation but, as dawn breaks and the cock crows, he remembers what Jesus had said, and he goes outside and weeps bitterly. Because the Jewish leaders can not put a man to death, a prerogative of the Romans, they bind Jesus and lead him away, and hand him over to Pilate, the Roman governor.

Judas is by now suffering remorse. He goes to the chief priests and elders and flings the thirty pieces of silver, the bribe money he had been paid to betray Jesus, at the their feet, and then goes out and hangs himself. Matthew adds that the chief priests use the tainted thirty pieces of silver to buy a potter's field which, having been bought with 'blood money' becomes known as the Field of Blood.

Back at Pilate's palace, Jesus stands before the governor who asks him, 'Are you the King of the Jews?' Jesus answers him. 'It is you who say it,' so confirming the truth spoken by Pilate. The chief priest and elders also accuse him but he offers no reply to any of their charges, and Pilate is amazed.

Pilate now tries a different tack. At festival time it was the governor's practice to release a prisoner for the people, and so he proposes to release the notorious prisoner Barabbas, because Pilate knows that Jesus has only been brought to him out of jealousy. As he is about to pronounce judgement, his wife sends him a message: 'Have nothing to do with that innocent man, for today I have suffered a great deal because of a dream about him.' Dreams, in Matthew's gospel, are a means of furnishing divine guidance.

However, the chief priests and elders persuade the crowd to have Barabbas released, and demand instead that Jesus be crucified. Pilate sees that he is making no impression and, afraid that a riot will ensue, washes his hands of the whole affair and declares his own innocence. 'I am innocent of this man's blood; see to it yourselves.' The people shout back, 'His blood, (his life), be on us and on our children!' It is important to note that this is a legal formula taking responsibility for the death of a person considered a criminal. It should not be seen, as later generations did, as implying that all Jews were responsible for the death of Jesus.

Pilate orders Jesus to be scourged, the normal Roman practice before crucifixion, and then handed over to be crucified. The Roman soldiers take Jesus into the Praetorium, probably the former palace of King Herod where Pilate was in residence during the Passover festival. The soldiers, in mockery, strip Jesus and make him put on a scarlet cloak, suggesting imperial purple, a crown of thorns and a reed in his right hand, suggesting a royal crown and sceptre. Making fun of Jesus, they address him as King of the Jews. Finally they put on his clothes and lead him away to be crucified.

On their way, they get one Simon from Cyrene, in present-day Libya, who was probably a pilgrim, to assist Jesus in carrying his cross. When they get to Golgotha, a name meaning Place of the Skull, the soldiers give him wine to drink mixed with gall but he refuses to drink it. Wine mixed with gall (myrrh) was a narcotic which sympathetic Jewish women used to offer to the condemned as a palliative. When the soldiers have crucified him, they divide his clothes among themselves;[12] then they sit down and keep watch over him.

They also crucify two bandits with him, while the passers-by taunt him, saying 'You who would destroy the temple and build it in three days, save yourself! If you are the Son of God, come down from the cross.' The chief priests, scribes and elders also mock him, saying, 'He saved others; he cannot save himself. He is the King of Israel; let him come down from the cross now, and we will believe in him. He trusts in God; let God deliver him now, if he wants to; for he said, "I am God's Son".'

---

12. A condemned man's clothes became the property of the executioners.

From noon on, darkness came over the whole land until the ninth hour, that is, from noon until three in the afternoon.[13] At about three, Jesus, in a mixture of Hebrew and Aramaic, cries out 'Eli, Eli, lama sabachthani?' that is, 'My God, my God, why have you forsaken me?'[14] Those standing by think that Jesus is calling on the prophet Elijah. One of them runs to get a sponge, fills it with vinegar, and puts it on a reed, and gives it to Jesus to drink. The others, no doubt hoping for a miracle, tell the one with the sponge to wait to see whether Elijah does come to save him. But Jesus again cries out in a loud voice, and breathes his last.

Matthew's reference to the 'darkness over the whole land' is a reference to the prophet Amos who had said that the Day of Yahweh would be accompanied by cosmic signs: 'On that day, says the Lord God, I will make the sun go down at noon, and darken the earth in broad daylight.'[15]

Matthew also tells us that at that moment of Jesus' death 'the curtain of the temple was torn in two, from top to bottom. The earth shook, and the rocks were split. The tombs were opened, and many bodies of the saints who had died were raised. After Jesus' resurrection, they came out of the tombs and entered the holy city and appeared to many. The centurion, together with those guarding Jesus, seeing the earthquake and all that was taking place, are terrified. The centurion says, "Truly this man was God's Son!"'

These signs and portents are Matthew's poetic and scriptural ways of describing the significance of Jesus' death. The tearing of the Temple curtain may well be a comment on the end of the old way of worshipping God or even of the Old Covenant. Matthew means that Temple worship in Jerusalem is at an end, as indeed it was by the time he wrote his gospel, and is now replaced by faith in Jesus Christ. The earthquakes and the opening of the tombs point to the future resurrection of God's faithful.

---

13. Amos 8:9
14. Jesus is quoting Psalm 22, a psalm of suffering, but also one of hope in God.
15. Amos 8:9

Just as many bodies of the saints were raised and, after the resurrection, appeared to many, so all will rise in the future to be with Jesus.[16]

Matthew mentions that many women were present at the crucifixion, looking on from a distance. They had followed Jesus from Galilee, and had provided for him. Among them were Mary Magdalene, and Mary the mother of James and Joseph, and the mother of the sons of Zebedee. These women witness Jesus' death and burial, and would later return to the tomb on Easter Sunday morning.

Joseph of Arimathea, a disciple, goes to Pilate and asks for Jesus' body, and prepares him for burial in his own tomb.[17] He then rolls a large stone across the entrance of the tomb and goes away. Mary of Magdalene and another Mary sit there opposite the sepulchre. Their function is not merely to act as mourners but as witnesses to the correct site where Jesus is buried. Since women's testimony was of little value in Jewish law, this detail is worthy of historical credence.

The chief priests and Pharisees ask Pilate to place a guard at the tomb because, they say, Jesus had stated that after three days he would rise from the dead. They are afraid that the disciples will come and steal the body, and then tell the people that Jesus had risen from the dead. Pilate agrees to their suggestion: Pilate says, 'You have a guard of soldiers; go and make the tomb secure as you can.' So they go with the guard and make the tomb secure by sealing the stone.

16. St Paul wrote, 'Christ has been raised from the dead, the first fruits of those who have died. For since death came through a human being, the resurrection of the dead has also come through a human being; for as all die in Adam, so all will be made alive in Christ.' (1 Corinthians 15:21)
17. Joseph's tomb would have been a cave designed for multiple burials laid out in bunk-like niches cut from the sides of the cave. In Jesus' day the corpse would have remained in the tomb for one year. Then the bones would be gathered and placed in a stone 'bone-box'. On the box the name or names of the deceased might be inscribed. Such a tomb could be used for entire families over several generations.

CHAPTER TWENTY-ONE

Resurrection
(28)

No one is reported as actually witnessing the resurrection of Jesus, and none of the gospel writers attempt to describe the event. They simply affirm that Jesus was raised to life by the Father, and not simply life as Jesus had lived it before, but to a different mode of existence. St Paul tries to make sense of what a raised body would be like when he writes about a 'spiritual' body, as opposed to a merely physical one, in his first Letter to the Corinthians.[1] With talk about resurrection we leave the realms of history, and enter into an event that is accessible only to those who have faith.

As far back as the first century AD, opponents of Christianity were claiming that the 'so-called resurrection' was fraudulent, that the disciples had stolen Jesus' body and had invented the various appearance stories. There were even claims that the women had gone to the wrong tomb, that Jesus' appearances were merely hallucinations, or that Jesus revived from only apparent death and wandered off on his own.

Some of the New Testament traditions, therefore, may be interpreted as countering such claims. Peter, in the Acts of the Apostles, is reported as saying, 'God raised him on the third day and allowed him to appear, not to all the people but to us who were chosen by God as witnesses, and who ate and drank with him after he rose from the dead.'[2] In Luke, the disciples thought they were seeing a ghost but Jesus showed them his wounded hands and feet and asked for something to eat.[3] There is even a stress on how, at first, the disciples did not believe what the

---

1. 1 Corinthians 15:35-54
2. Acts 10:41
3. Luke 24:41-43

women, who came running from the tomb, told them. Even when he appeared to the eleven disciples in Galilee, Matthew tells us, some hesitated.

Each Evangelist writes from within a different tradition, so they vary on the circumstances and details of Christ's various appearances. Some refer to appearances in Jerusalem, others to appearances in Galilee.[4] All have reference to Christ appearing to the eleven apostles. What was important for each evangelist was testimony that a well-known apostolic figure, known to his community, had seen Jesus.

Matthew's description of the resurrection event is quite brief, consisting only of three short paragraphs. On the day after the Sabbath, and towards dawn on the first day of the week, Mary of Magdalene and the other Mary, the mother of James and Joseph, go to Jesus' tomb. Suddenly there is a violent earthquake; an angel of the Lord, descending from heaven, rolls back the stone at the mouth of the tomb, and sits on it. His appearance is like lightening, his clothing white as snow. One is reminded of the transfigured Jesus.[5]

Matthew's description is probably influenced by words taken from the prophets. Cosmic signs, earthquakes and a solar eclipse accompany the day of Yahweh, the day of God's triumph. Isaiah, for example, had written, 'Get among the rocks, hide in the dust at the sight of the terror of Yahweh, at the brilliance of his majesty, when he arises to make the earth quake.'[6] Matthew's imagery, of course, is not to be taken literally.

The guards are so shaken, so frightened of the angel, or of the young man in Mark's gospel[7] that they are like dead men. But the angel says to the women, 'Do not be afraid; I know that you are looking for Jesus who was crucified. He is not here; for he has been raised, as he said. Come see the place where he lay.

---

4. Appearances in Jerusalem are to be found in Luke, John and Mark. Appearances in Galilee are to be found in Matthew, and John.
5. Matthew 17:2
6. Isaiah 2:10
7. Mark 16:5

Then go quickly and tell his disciples, 'He has been raised from the dead, and indeed he is going ahead of you to Galilee; there you will see him. This is my message for you.' Filled with fear and great joy, the women quickly leave the tomb and run to tell the disciples. This interesting comment seems credible because women's testimony would have beeen discountable in rabbinic law.

While they are on their way, Jesus suddenly meets them. 'Greetings!' he says. They come to him, take hold of his feet, and worship him. Jesus says to them, 'Do not be afraid; go and tell my brothers that they must go to Galilee; there they will see me.' By calling his disciples brothers, Jesus indicates that they are forgiven for deserting him in his hour of need.

Matthew now goes on to describe the actions of some of the guards at Jesus' tomb. They go off to tell the chief priests all that had happened. A meeting is held and, after some discussion, the soldiers are handed a considerable sum of money and instructed to say that during the night the disciples came and stole Jesus' body while they were asleep. The elders also tell them that if the governor comes to hear about what had happened, they would put things right with him themselves, making sure that they did not get into trouble. Matthew speaks about a cover up: 'The soldiers took the money and did as they were directed. And this is still told among the Jews to this day.'

Finally Matthew writes about Christ's appearance to the eleven in Galilee. The disciples go to a mountain where Jesus has arranged to meet them. When they see him they worship him; but, Matthew says, some doubted. Why? Was it simply because of the seeming impossibility of such an occurrence? At any rate Jesus comes and says to them, 'All authority in heaven and on earth has been given to me. Go, therefore and make disciples of all the nations, baptising them in the name of the Father and of the Son and of the Holy Spirit, and teaching them to obey everything that I have commanded you. And remember, I am with you always, to the end of the age.'

Mathew's mountain setting for this appearance recalls the

scenes where Moses received the Ten Commandments,[8] the mountain where Jesus spoke about the Beatitudes[9] and the scene of the Transfiguration.[10]

Jesus speaking about all authority being given to him recalls the words of the prophet Daniel, 'on him was conferred sovereignty, glory and kingship, and all peoples, nations and languages became his servants. His sovereignty is an eternal sovereignty which will never pass away, nor will his empire every be destroyed.'[11]

The command, to 'make disciples of all nations' revises the restriction that Jesus had imposed on the disciples earlier in the gospel: 'Go nowhere among the gentiles, and enter no towns of the Samaritans, but go rather to the lost sheep of the House of Israel.'[12] By the time Matthew wrote his gospel, Gentiles and Samaritans were already members of the Christian community.

Jesus' injunction to baptise 'in the name of the Father and of the Son and of the Holy Spirit' appears nowhere else in the New Testament. It is probably a reflection of the liturgical usage established much later in the primitive community. When he commands them to 'Teach them to observe all the commands I gave you', Matthew is probably referring to all that he has related in his gospel.

Jesus final comment, 'Remember, I am with you always, to the end of the age' refers back to what the angelic messenger said in chapter one; 'The virgin shall conceive and bear a son, and they shall name him Emmanuel, which means "God is with us".' The risen Christ is the divine presence with his people, assisting them in their prayer, study, teaching, their baptising and preaching. In John's gospel these attributes are assigned to God's Spirit, or, as St Paul would say, the Spirit of Christ.

Saint Paul once wrote, 'If Christ has not been raised, then our

---

8. Exodus 19:20
9. Matthew 5:1
10. Matthew 17:1
11. Daniel 7:14
12. Matthew 10:5-6

proclamation has been in vain and your faith has been in vain.'[13] But is resurrection from the dead really credible? A former Cambridge Professor of Mathematical Physics, John Polkinghorne, has this to say about the idea of resurrection:

> Clearly, such an idea goes beyond our direct experience but it seems to me in no way to run counter to it. There is nothing particularly important in the actual physical constituents of our bodies. After a few years' nutrition, and wear and tear the atoms that make us up have nearly all been replaced by equivalent successors. It is the pattern they form which constitutes the physical expression of our continuing personality. There seems no difficulty in conceiving of that pattern, dissolved in death, being recreated in another environment in an act of resurrection. In terms of a crude analogy, it would be like transforming the software of a computer programme (the 'pattern' of our personality) from one piece of hardware (our body in this world) to another (our body in the world to come.) Scientifically this seems a coherent idea.[14]

Werner Von Braun, who more than any other scientist was responsible for putting Americans on the moon, gave this testimony before he died concerning life after death. 'I think that science has a real surprise for the sceptics … nothing in nature, not even the tiniest particle, can disappear without trace. Nature does not know extinction. All it knows is transformation. Everything that science has taught me – and continues to teach me – strengthens my belief in the continuity of our spiritual existence after death.'

Whatever about science, the gospels make the point that faith in the risen Christ will only make sense to those who have a loving relationship with him. The important questions are always the same: Do you believe? Do you love? Are you a disciple? If so, you have eternal life in Christ.

---

13. 1Corinthians 15:14
14. *One World: The Interaction of Science and Theology*, SPCK 1993

CHAPTER TWENTY-TWO

Inspiration

What do people mean when they say that the Bible is the inspired word of God? Perhaps the best place to start is with the definition given by the bishops at the second Vatican Council:

> Those things revealed by God which are contained and presented in the text of sacred scripture have been written under the inspiration of the Holy Spirit. For holy mother church, relying on the faith of the apostolic age, accepts as sacred and canonical the books of the Old and the New Testaments, whole and entire, with all their parts on the grounds that, written under the inspiration of the Holy Spirit, they have God as their author, and have been handed on as such to the church itself. To compose the sacred books, God chose certain men who, all the while he employed them in this task, made full use of their powers and faculties, so that, though he acted in them and by them, it was as true authors that they consigned to writing whatever he wanted written, and no more.
>
> Since, therefore, all that the inspired authors, or sacred writers, affirm should be regarded as affirmed by the Holy Spirit, we must acknowledge that the books of scripture, firmly, faithfully and without error, teach that truth which God, for the sake of our salvation, wished to see confided to the sacred scriptures. Thus 'All scripture is inspired by God, and is useful for teaching, for reproof, for correction and for training in righteousness, so that everyone who belongs to God may be proficient, equipped for every good work.' (2 Timothy 3:16-17)

To tease out the implications of what Vatican Two was saying about inspiration it is important to remember that the Bible is made up of a collection of some 70 books of different literary genres, written at different times, and in different places, over a period of a thousand years. The Bible is rather like a library of collected works, gathered together in one place.

Some people think that everything written in the Bible is history and is to be taken literally. This is simply not the case. The Bible also contains inspired poetry, drama, legend, fiction etc. For example, the first chapters of the Book of Genesis would not be classified in the branch of the Biblical library called 'science', but in the branch called 'religious lore and legends'. We don't have to accept the Genesis description of the creation of the world as a scientific account. Rather, it is an account that the author(s) took from the various legends of surrounding peoples to make the 'inspired' point that God alone is the creator of all that exists.

If the Book of Jonah is a parable and not history, then God's inspiration makes it an inspired parable. The truth that it tries to convey is that God desires people to acknowledge God as God, and lead a moral way of life. Inspiration does not mean believing that a historical figure named Jonah was swallowed by a big fish.

As the Vatican Council said, the Old and New Testaments have been committed to writing under the inspiration of the Holy Spirit. But 'in composing the sacred books, God chose men and, while employed by him, they made use of their powers and abilities, so with him acting in them and through them, they, as true authors, consigned to writing everything and only those things which he wanted.'

God inspires the biblical authors to write 'that truth which God wanted to put into the sacred writings for the sake of our salvation.' This does not mean that everything written in the Bible is pure history. Whether the human author is using poetry (the Psalms), parables (Jonah and the Parables of Jesus), legends, (the creation story in Genesis), he is using his own powers and abilities to convey some truth that God wishes to convey that leads to our salvation, to our union with God in love. God's inspiration of the Bible does not make irrelevant the outlook and personal situation of the human author. God knows all things, but the human author does not; and biblical authors do not have answers for all human questions.

Questions about inspiration often arise because of the views of those atheists who deny the existence of God, and therefore deny divine inspiration as having any reality, and, more commonly, the views expressed by those who are called fundamentalists.

Fundamentalism as a modern phenomenon arose in the United States somewhere around 1910 due, in no small part to what is called historical criticism. The term can be misleading in that, in English, the word criticism often involves negative judgements. Biblical criticism is of a different kind. It means a careful reading and analysis of a biblical text so that one comes to understand it more completely. One tries to understand the author's background, his personal situation, and the purpose of his writing. Biblical criticism also seeks to understand the audience to whom the work was addressed: Who were they? Where were they? What were their problems? Would they have understood what the author meant? In other words, biblical criticism asks the same type of questions about a biblical book that one would ask about any other book.

However, in querying the books of the Bible in the same way as one queries any other book, God's word can become obscured, especially if the enquirer does not have a firm faith in the Bible's divine origin. This is why two wealthy Southern Californians paid for a series of pamphlets to defend the fundamentals of Christian belief, namely doctrines such as Jesus' virginal conception, the miracles of Jesus, the resurrection, and so on. These pamphlets, while well intended, also had an anti-evolutionary view of creation which remains common today among many fundamentalists in the United States.

The difference between Roman Catholics and fundamentalists lies in the fact that the latter try to prove Christian doctrines with the understanding that the only way to do so is to maintain the literal meaning of everything written in the Bible. As one Catholic scholar has pointed out, 'A literalist reading of the Bible is intellectually indefensible and is quite unnecessary for the defence of the basic Christians doctrines.'

It is my hope that *Matthew* will enable those who read and meditate on the gospel to have a better understanding of what sort of document it is. As John's gospel says, the words were written so that 'you may come to believe that Jesus in the Messiah, the Son of God, and that through believing you may have life in his name.'